ESSENCES OF NATURE

Essences of Nature

Botanical Remedies for Growth and Empowerment

Mary Ann Altamirano Antenucci, CH, CSC

Light Technology Publishing

* * *

ISBN-13: 978-1-62233-006-5

Light Technology Publishing, LLC
Phone: 800-450-0985
928-526-1345
Fax: 928-714-1132
PO Box 3540
Flagstaff, AZ 86003
www.lighttechnology.com

Contents

Preface

Flower essences have been described in various ways: liquid drops of consciousness, vibrational essences, a means to resonate with your higher self, liquid light treatments, the fifth element, soul helpers, and reminders of what we could be if we allowed ourselves to truly blossom. Flower essences are friends. They work by gently nudging you to be a better you. They hold up what can be possible and then energetically strive to get you there. Flower essences can get you out of your way. You might have many fears that could limit you from the life you imagine you can have. They don't make the fears evaporate but inject you with the courage to face them, empowering you to meet your challenges.

My first experience with flower essences was when I was researching a paper on spontaneous remission. I was in my senior seminar and was thrilled to be in an alternative medicine, or holistic health, class. I thought I knew a lot about alternative health due to my own struggles with asthma and allergies. I had severe environmental allergies and trouble breathing. Plants and flowers made me wheeze and sneeze.

Flower Power

I came across a phrase about the power of flower therapy and questioned the seriousness of such a modality. I believe I laughed at how flowers could heal considering how they made my life miserable. Later that week, I was shopping at one of our local food co-ops, similar to a down-scaled version of Whole Foods, and spotted a book on flower essences: *Bach Flower Remedies* by Philip Chancellor. I randomly opened the book to the page about Holly.

Holly is indicated for hate, frustration, anger, and not feeling unconditional love. At the time, I was frustrated and going through much personal discord; I was a pregnant, starving student with a demanding work and home life. In general, I was not feeling the love. All of the symptoms matched my current state and the system made sense to me. I liked the idea that instead of confronting, controlling, and combating my emotional state, I was able to shift to the opposite spectrum of whatever emotion I was experiencing. There was ease to this method.

I then bought a bottle of Holly. I followed the directions and felt an immediate sense of peace. Not the peace of meditation or napping, but the peace that comes from being supported just as you are.

Over the next few months, I purchased many of the set of Bach's thirty-eight essences and pored over all the information that was available. My bibles were *The Medical Discoveries of Edward Bach* by Nora Weeks, *Bach Flower Remedies* by Philip Chancellor, and *The Flower Essence Repertory* by Richard Katz and Patricia Kaminski.

I loved the way flower essences helped to address the underlying cause of imbalance and disease. I understood how the flowers worked by helping to realize our potential. I was enthusiastic (very Vervain) and took it upon myself to start transforming family and friends. I was thrilled about how you could feel the energetic shifts almost immediately. The flowers picked me.

I found that flower essences raised our personal vibrations. I liken it to changing our bandwidth. It's as if we know we need them when the way we are operating is not working for us or we need an upgrade. Most of us are still stuck in the dial-up mentality of Internet years gone by. We want to get online to access all the parts and experiences that we know are readily available. However, we may get stuck when trying to navigate and become disconnected — and disappointed. We know what we want is there, but we feel it may no longer be accessible to us or maybe the post has been removed.

The flowers helped me to grow. I also noticed the people I shared these essences with — who had been living in the good old days of their pasts — now embracing new opportunities. I witnessed long-standing broken hearts healed and cleansed. I saw dark clouds of gloom and doom lift, revealing sparks of light and hope. I saw fears and phobias turn into challenges of courage and personal empowerment. I saw the way these people communicated with one another change as it became softer with more clarity and more authentic feelings. I saw passion restored to an apathetic soul. I saw skeletal changes, as these people were now able to stand up straight and stand their ground.

My intention for this book is to be a friend, guide, and resource to you. This book is the compilation of my columns over the past decade. I wish it to be the go-to place when you are in need of a shift in energy. Flower essences are living energies, and I know that they can bring more vigor and vitality to your life. My interpretations of the flower essences are often tailored to fit the needs of a particular circumstance. The book has been formatted with keywords for quick reference to whatever issues you would like to explore. I also want you to use the book intuitively: Ask a question and open to a page that gives you exactly what you need.

Introduction

Flower essences are often confused with aromatherapy and essential oils. These all are derived from plants and flowers and have emotional and energetic properties, but that is where the similarities end. In general, aromatherapy works on your physical senses: It soothes, calms and energizes. The primary sense used with this therapy is the sense of smell. Essential oils are made by distilling plant material into pure oil. Flower essences work on the emotional and etheric bodies, or the body double, and they activate our energies by enhancing the positive. They have no fragrance except for the smell of whatever they may be preserved in at the time.

The flower essence formula is made from picking flowers at their peak. The blossom is then immersed in pure spring water in a clear bowl and placed under the clear, sunny sky for four to six hours. This water holds the memory of the flower, which is then preserved by adding brandy or apple cider vinegar. This is called the mother tincture. The mother tincture is then further diluted for use in a stock formula. The stock formula is the most common way we work with the essences. Flower essences are generally made into formulas to be ingested, added to bath water, or sprayed in the air. Each delivery system is effective, as the essence works on the emotional and etheric bodies, not specifically on the physical body.

High Vibrations

The flower is the highest vibration of the plant. All the energy and potential of the plant is contained in the flower or the bud. Through the flower, all of the life force and possibility is activated in the energies of the plant. Each type of flower has its own signature. Depending on the specific configuration of the plant — bell, cup, or star — its flower can work on physical, emotional, or spiritual states of being. For example, bell-shaped flowers tend to be helpful with earthly and physical issues, cup-shaped flowers help us to receive, and star-shaped flowers tend to be used for spiritual issues or issues for which we get our inspiration from the divine.

The flower's signature is further developed by its location as well as its color, physical appearance, axis, and specific botanical properties.

Flower essences work through the process of resonance. Think about times when you needed to have roses or you couldn't get enough sunflowers or you needed to be around irises: There was something about that particular flower that you needed to have in your space. The nature of the flower was directly speaking to your psyche about a correction you needed. By the way, irises are for inspiration, and roses get the life forces going again by bringing passion back into our lives. Sunflowers activate your radiance and self-esteem. If a particular essence isn't the right one for you at the time, nothing will change; it just won't work. Flower essences are very safe and gentle and will not interfere with any other modalities, such as supplements, energy work, medications, and so on.

Essences for All Reasons

There are certain flower essences that I call the universal essences. These particular essences can benefit anyone who uses them. They are made from holly, wild oat, and mariposa lily.

Holly is the essence for love — love of self and love for others. It embodies the concept of unconditional love. Holly essence works on the principle of raising any negative vibration to that of love and connection. Traditionally, it is used for strong negative emotions, such as hate and envy, or any emotion that causes us to shrink and lock ourselves in. It is one of the remedies that also act as a catalyst for change. When we feel as if we are operating from a hard shell that nothing can penetrate, holly essence can work its miracle by softening the inner core of the heart.

Wild oat essence is a catalyst for growth. It is the remedy to get us unstuck. It is traditionally used for people who can do many things but master none — jacks-of-all-trades. This remedy is for those moments when we ask, "What is the choice or path I should take for my life?" "Where am I best served, and what are my real talents?" Wild oat clears the way. It gives direction. It is a great remedy for the times we can't decide what to do first. It has a prioritizing effect on what we should do next, allowing us to activate movement and clarity.

Finally, mariposa lily is one of my all-time-favorite universal essences. I love it because it teaches us to love ourselves the mother-love way: unconditional, sweet, and precious. From the perspective of this love, we can do no wrong. A little mothering goes a long way, and we all could use that touch of love.

Resources for "Higher" Living

A saying that keeps popping into my mind is, "It's time to use all the tools in the toolbox!" With everything going on in our lives and our attention diverted in so many directions, it becomes easy to forget that we have what we need at any given moment. How many times have we been with a friend or a coworker or commiserating with someone about our current state of affairs and that person mentions a solution we had already thought of but discounted for some reason — or even forgot?

There is a card in the tarot called the Four of Cups, and in my particular deck, it depicts a man sitting on a giant cup, which looks like a stool, while mulling over the empty little cup in his hand. He is sitting on his "assets" and putting his attention on how little or what is not there. Let us not sit on our assets.

Flower essences help us to achieve our highest vibrations. They do it softly and gently but with persistence. They awaken the sleeping giant of our highest possibilities. Flower essences help us to remember who we are and assist us in being our best selves. We grow by being, and we do it with smiles on our faces and with a knowing in our hearts. Enjoy being you.

CHAPTER ONE

Cosmic Cleansers

We can embrace change, or we can fear change. The more we try to keep things manageable, the more we stifle our own growth. Embrace change and transformation: grow, change, radiate, create, procreate, and celebrate. Harness the power of transition to transform now. Be the change you want to achieve.

Apple Blossom

Apple blossom essence is a purification essence. It helps by getting to the core of who we are and cutting away noxious influences from the past as it clears contaminants from the energy field. As our systems become cleaner and clearer, we have more energy for making new thoughts, feeling new feelings, and seeing new possibilities. Apple blossom essence restores hope. It helps us to move beyond perceived limitations, reminding us of the star qualities we possess. This remedy instills peace in our hearts so that we are no longer hindered by our stories or the remnants of past lives. Through apple blossom's influence, we are new, fresh, and able as we proceed in peace.

Quick Reference

- Gets to our core
- Clears the past
- Restores hope
- Aids purification
- Instills peace

Baby Blue Eyes

Baby blue eyes works by helping us to overcome insecurity and distrust. It helps us during those moments when we find that we are defensive and waiting for the other shoe to drop, when we can't relax or enjoy anything at all because we are constantly thinking about or preparing for the

Quick Reference

- Restores innocence
- Inspires trust
- Helps overcome insecurity
- Eases cynicism

worst-case scenario. When we no longer have trust or faith in something greater than us, we feel that we can depend only on ourselves, resulting in a deep loneliness and isolation.

Baby blue eyes restores our innocence and the trust in something greater than ourselves. It freshens up the soul. When using baby blue eyes, we feel we can take that first step of allowing trust and acceptance again. We feel goodness as a viable possibility in our lives.

Beech

Beech essence is the beast or "b@$%" essence. It is used for irritation and harsh judgment. There are times when we just can't stand what others are saying or doing and we think that we can do it better. Or maybe we find that we can't get out of our own way because of our perception of how we think things should be. The indication that this essence is needed is when everything and everyone is an irritant and we react harshly.

Quick Reference

- Builds tolerance
- Soothes hypersensitivity
- Balances judgment
- Softens harshness
- Fosters acceptance

This essence helps us by creating boundaries from the place of being centered and grounded rather than creating barriers of attitude and hostility. Beech essence is the remedy for helping us with understanding and acceptance. It is great for allergies and physical irritations as well. It helps us create a shield of calm and confidence by reestablishing an inner sanctuary. This formula makes it safe to be ourselves. Beech essence acts as a Band-Aid for the bratty and the bitchy.

The more we can be accepting of others, the more we can be accepting of ourselves — and vice versa. Beech essence helps us to accept and embrace everything about others as well as all of ourselves. Rather than feeling distanced from people or disgusted by them, we feel connected and compassionate. We embrace the beauty and power of difference. We satisfy the itch of irritation by soothing ourselves and our surroundings with acceptance and kindness.

Beech essence has the ability to soothe the tendency to control, which leads to an intriguing effect on allergies. On an energetic level, many allergies are adverse reactions to external forces or forces beyond our control — in other words, oversensitivity to our personal environments. The beech essence helps us to modify the need to control and has the effect of relaxing the body's systems overall. Beech encourages us to build tolerance. Tolerance allows us to flow and be more in harmony. It warms the soul, allowing us to build acceptance of others and ourselves.

The positive outcome of working with beech is a new tolerance: a tolerance for ourselves, such as a good mother would demonstrate, as well as a tolerance for others. This essence can help us feel the love despite whatever problems might exist. It helps us to see our own value as well as the value of others. We feel the grand plan evolve and see how each of us contributes in our own particular way. We learn to use our hypervigilance and judgment to provide productive and insightful guidance.

Beech

Chaparral

Chaparral

Chaparral essence is for cleansing emotional and psychic debris. Its job is to provide a filtering system for all the toxic input we receive. Often we don't realize how much negativity, doubt, and wear and tear we are exposed to. The expectation of the debris becomes the norm for us, as in the outlook that "_____ happens," and the more that "_____ happens," the more we tend to expect and attract that expectation. This essence protects us from such an assault on the senses. It balances psychic and emotional awareness. Chaparral creates and cleanses by eliminating all the cosmic clutter that no longer serves us.

Quick Reference

- Works as psychic filter
- Purifies emotional debris
- Cleanses disturbed dreams
- Balances awareness
- Helps with drug detoxification

Have you ever seen a movie that affected you in an extremely negative way, and as a result, you were not able to remove a certain image or thought process from your mind? We are inundated with imagery on a daily basis. Whether we are conscious of it or not, there is a trend that causes us to question who we are and where we fit in the grand scheme of things. We are bombarded by images and experiences that lower our vibration.

Chaparral essence is an effective astral filter for the impressionable. It is the great detoxifier. We can think about it as spring-cleaning for both our psyches and our physical bodies. It is a powerful and effective cleanser, aiding in any detoxification or fasting program. This essence helps us to realize where the distortions in our realities are and how to correct them. Chaparral is great for dream work and, in particular, for lucid dreaming in which we begin to have mastery over the images of our dreams, which can carry over to mastery in our waking lives.

This essence is an energy cleanser with psychic cleansing properties. It helps us to release negative and disturbing images from our consciousnesses. It also has a protective quality, as it creates a psychic filter for the many competing issues that we face. Chaparral helps us to break down and digest our experiences for processing. It also helps us to deal with the chaos. It helps us by sorting out what we need to pay attention to and what psychic-system overload is. Chaparral helps us to clear and move forward.

Cherry Plum

Cherry plum is known as the "out of control" essence. It is usually used when we are afraid of losing control — when we strive to measure our reactions and strictly control our environments so the fear won't show or creep through. It is for those times when we want to react to that guy who cuts us off by plowing into his car with a tank, or when we feel we might ultimately pass out from trying to hold on so tightly. Cherry plum essence helps us to get a grip. It pulls us back from the brink of our own disasters. Cherry plum helps by letting

Quick Reference

- Helps get a grip
- Addresses fear of losing control
- Taps into courage
- Restores trust
- Accesses inner guidance

Cherry Plum

us take the reins over our fears. With its assistance, we can learn how to manage those fears and emotions. We realize that it is normal, even advisable, to express our emotions and fears — and therefore not to be ruled by them. Cherry plum essence helps us to create the change from out-of-control fear and chaos to self-management.

This is the remedy for when you reach your breaking point, no matter how much you've tried to hold it together. The interesting aspect of cherry plum essence is that it addresses the fear of losing control rather than the action of losing control. This degree of fear shuts off our access to guidance and reason and the ability to see the bigger picture. This essence helps us to gain clarity by clearing the fear of fear.

Cherry plum is the fourth component of the Rescue Remedy formula (see Special Combinations chapter). When we don't feel safe to express ourselves and we try to fit in or go along with the status quo, cherry plum helps us to tap into our courage. It helps us to be in the flow of events. It works by assisting in releasing the pent-up trauma and drama. With this essence, we can access our inner guidance. We feel the peace of our choices and are no longer consumed by the fear of losing control. We feel strong enough to trust. We feel safe and composed.

Corn

Quick Reference

- Connects to environment
- Creates inner spaciousness
- Connects to universe
- Imparts sense of belonging

Corn essence is a way of reconnecting with Mother Earth. When we feel surrounded by concrete and technology, it is difficult to feel our parts in the cosmos. We may feel more like a part of the cement than anything else. Corn essence helps us to feel our roots — literally. It gives us a deeper appreciation of where we came from, and it helps us to sense our parts in nature, even if our experience of nature is a city park or grass growing out of the cracks in the asphalt.

This is a grounding essence. It imparts a sense of belonging and value in the grand scheme of things. It is a practical essence, used to make us feel more real to ourselves. Corn essence shows us how to be connected to the universe despite our circumstances and physical environments.

Corn

Crab Apple

Crab apple essence is the traditional emotional, physical, and psychological cleanser. We can use this essence when we feel ill or when our environment is contaminated by either toxins or toxic thoughts. This remedy's key applications are cleansing and putting issues in perspective. All of the fretting and chastising we do can only get us so far. We can only wash our hands so many times before we irritate and injure our skin. Crab apple helps us to remember that order is a temporary state. Order and cleanliness come from being mindful, watching our thoughts and deeds, and appreciating and fully participating in our lives. After we cleanse, we can create with new perspective.

Quick Reference

- Cleanses emotions, body, psyche
- Eases OCD tendencies
- Helps us relax and accept
- Clears old patterns
- Helps with detoxification

This is the remedy used for the times we are making mountains out of molehills. It is good for the times we work harder to correct a problem, but the problem has a way of getting bigger and bigger. It might begin as the tiniest scratch on the car, and we rub it until all the paint is dull and exposed, creating a much bigger mess that ultimately needs a more extensive repair. But we just can't leave well enough alone!

There is a reason why crab apple is one of the components of the famous Rescue Remedy formula (see Special Combinations chapter): It treats impurities of all types and helps to reduce the fear of being around anxiety-producing substances. People with obsessive-compulsive disorders have had great success with crab apple. It helps the soul to relax and accept. Crab apple is a big-picture formula. When we are caught up in all the minutiae, it broadens our scope so that we can see and feel what is really important. Rather than needing to have everything in perfect order to feel a degree of control, we can relax into the notion that everything is already in perfect order at any given time.

We can also use crab apple essence to clear the effects of old patterns and stagnant modalities. Crab apple assists in realigning and balancing the subtle bodies. This essence works on what is taking up the most space in our minds and needs to be defragmented. Whether it is our concept of how things are supposed to be or a focus on cleanliness of the body, all details can become amplified. Sometimes there tends to be so much mental energy devoted to how to "correct" and "cleanse," the problem becomes a never-ending cycle.

To challenge any obstacle, it is important to be clear — to know what the challenge really is. Crab apple essence clears all of our energy bodies for a fresh start. It clears the impurities from negative thought forms. It clears the physical energy from stagnant processes. Crab apple essence

Crab Apple

helps with any physical or emotional detoxification we are going through. It allows us to become fortified because we are that much clearer.

During the holiday season, we are around more people than usual, and some are coughing and sneezing. We might feel that we don't want to connect because of exposure and contamination. We could have toxic emotions that come through due to family get-togethers and their social patterns. We can get out of balance because our family relations are out of balance. Crab apple essence helps us to cleanse what doesn't work for us, whether it is emotional or physical. It works for colds, the flu, allergies, and even detox programs. Try using this essence during the next holiday season as your first-line defense for whatever toxic exposures or emotions happen to arise. You just might find that you are starting the holidays with a clean slate and you're able to truly enjoy the sharing of spirit.

Echinacea

Quick Reference

- Restores sense of self
- Heals soul connections
- Breaks addictive patterns
- Provides hope, emotional backup
- Creates a new "core"

Echinacea essence works when there has been a physical, spiritual, or emotional assault to the sense of self. There are so many modern factors that can disrupt our connection to our higher selves and spirituality, and Echinacea heals our soul connections. It helps to rebuild our energy fields and our connections to our core.

This remedy challenges us by restoring our sense of self and purpose. It moves us beyond our limitations, beyond what has happened to us, and helps weave together the sum of all our experiences. Echinacea essence frees us by redefining who we are at a core level. It is the essence we use for picking up the pieces and putting them back together again when we have bottomed out. It is perfect for treating the feeling of being shattered. We can lose our core selves because of serious trauma or abuse, and that very spark that defines us can get broken into a million pieces.

This remedy works when we feel that nothing else will. It helps us to create a new sense of self. It allows us to learn how to restore and recenter to true authenticity. When we feel that our integrity has been

either threatened or disseminated, when we feel that we are not the same anymore because of what we have been through, or when we lose our sense of self or our faith in what can still be, Echinacea essence can be very curative. It helps to provide the spark of hope in the midst of extreme challenges. It provides the emotional backup to replenish our foundations. It helps us to feel intact again.

Elm

Quick Reference

- Instills moderation
- Manages unreasonable expectations
- Lends confidence
- Eases symptoms of overload

Elm essence is for those times when we feel overwhelmed and overloaded by all of the demands on our time and attention. This is a good formula to use when we reach the straw that breaks the camel's back. It is perfect for the times when we can't possibly do one more thing, when we feel we can't keep up anymore, and when we feel like abject failures. Elm essence reminds us to pace ourselves. It helps us remember that we are not alone and that help is there for us. This is the "let go and let God" essence. It helps us align with our higher selves to feel the support for all of our abilities. It also helps us let go of the feeling that we are letting others down and not living up to our own expectations. Elm essence lends the core confidence to transcend our burdens and enter a realm of peace and productivity.

Irritation and allergies are often symptoms of overload. We need elm when we feel inadequate and not up to the task of living. It is used for those times when we feel we are on top of things but the slightest situation tips the balance. It's for those times when so much is going on and we are juggling all those plates in the air so well, but then, at the slightest distraction, everything comes tumbling down. Oh no! We no longer have our natural defenses and everything seems problematic.

Elm essence helps us to learn that we are not simply what we do. It breaks the cycle of thinking that how much we do defines how much we are. It encourages us to set a different pace. It teaches us that being perfect is following our natural rhythms. Elm is restorative and puts us back into balance: It puts Humpty Dumpty together again, allowing us to cope better. It helps us to spring into action with some tools for change and empowerment and reminds us how wonderful we are. Elm incites feelings of warmth, invigoration, and restoration.

Elm

Filaree

Filaree

Quick Reference

- Finds where we're stuck
- Shows the bigger picture
- Channels mental energy
- Promotes discernment
- Increases productivity, balance

Filaree essence is indicated for obsessive worry, for those times when we find ourselves just focusing on what can go wrong. When we feel out of control during catastrophic events, we can find ourselves doing weird and superstitious things to stave off fear. We may fuss over the little details of what needs to go to the laundry and not take care of the leak in the sink that needs to be fixed, which is probably of more immediate concern. When there is a loss of perspective, filaree essence gives overview, allowing us to see where we become stuck or obsessed. We can break away from the microview and see the big picture, no longer distracted by the details.

This essence works by sorting out what is important and what isn't. It helps us to stop being so enmeshed in the list of things to do. It frees our energy from what we "should" do and what "needs" to be done, allowing us to ask, "How will this fit into the big picture?" It promotes discernment over distraction. We can liberate our natural talents by knowing our personal priorities. Filaree helps us to become more productive as we gain insight and achieve the perfection of balance.

Fireweed

Fireweed

Fireweed essence is known as the fire remedy. When we are being tested in the most intense manner, this remedy can help us to rise from the ashes. It burns away excessive emotions and attachments, allowing us to feel our authentic selves discovered or returning. This essence is regenerative and restorative.

Fireweed works well for any healing crisis. It helps us to rebuild by getting in touch with the essence of who we are. Fireweed is used for deep damage to the body, the earth, and the psyche. We are able to begin again with renewed energy and purified qualities. We are cleansed, purified, and transformed through our experiences.

Quick Reference

- Regenerates and restores
- Aids in reclaiming vitality
- Promotes healing from catastrophe
- Accelerates personal growth

Garlic

Garlic essence restores and bolsters the auric field. It addresses weakness caused by too many negative thought forms or outside energetic influences. This is the essence for combating the effects of psychic vampires. It also works well for lowered vitality caused by viral or parasitic disturbances as well as sudden spiritual openings. This essence works when we are in a state of deficiency and don't have enough vitality to naturally fend for ourselves. It protects by unifying the auric fields.

Quick Reference

- Fortifies energy systems
- Raises low vitality
- Creates a natural defense system
- Restores unity
- Protects energy bodies

Garlic essence is known as a fortifying formula. It promotes physical healing and helps us with our natural resistances to outside influences. It is traditionally used when our subtle energy forces become scattered and torn due to a constant barrage of mental and emotional attacks, leaving our auras worse for the wear and tear. Garlic essence helps by rallying the forces of active resistance, creating a natural defense system that filters out aberrant influences. Garlic reestablishes the connection between all the energy bodies. Peace comes again from the unifying wholeness and active protection this essence provides.

Garlic

Gentian

Gentian

Gentian is the essence for self-doubt and discouragement. All of us stumble, fall, and skin our knees at times, but our ability to get up, dust ourselves off, and start walking — or even running — again is what keeps us moving. It reminds us to not let ourselves be defined by discouragement and defeat.

Quick Reference

- Overcomes doubt
- Instills trust, faith, confidence
- Renews sense of purpose
- Encourages resilience

Gentian is sometimes regarded as the setback essence. This remedy instills trust and faith in our confidence and abilities. It lends resilience, mental agility, and creativity to our challenges. We learn that mishaps and obstacles are often tools for change, problem solving, and success. Gentian essence helps us to spring forward by leaping over the challenges of discouragement and self-doubt.

Say we are going along, feeling on track and on top of the world, and then "kaboom!" our world as we know it falls apart. What do we do? Disappointments can and will stifle us if we let them. Gentian addresses the disappointments and lack of faith. It moves us beyond them so we can look at the bigger picture and put these roadblocks in perspective. Gentian helps us see them as challenges — nothing more. We begin to trust that it will all work out in the most mysterious of ways.

Sometimes we get knocked around. We forget what we know. We forget how to get there, and we forget how far we have already come. Gentian essence restores the energetic battery necessary to work around the plan when the plan isn't working anymore. Whether we are experiencing a health crisis or a financial crisis, this is the remedy for when we feel we are at the end of the line. Gentian essence renews our sense of purpose and destiny. It reconnects us to the possibilities of life's plan. This remedy reminds us to find hope and optimism again, letting the miracles happen.

Goldenrod

Quick Reference

- Fosters authenticity
- Strengthens personal power
- Balances opposing demands
- Eases need for approval

Goldenrod is known as the "playing to the crowd" essence. It the remedy for tailoring who we are according to what others expect us to be. Goldenrod essence manages our individuality. It is for those who strive to be the person others need them to be and thus can lose their identities in personal performance. Goldenrod helps by making it safe to be ourselves in whatever group or circumstance we choose. With its help, we get to be ourselves. We see how we contribute to the group by being stronger individuals in a group setting. Goldenrod essence allows us to be the living representation of our authenticity.

There are times when we feel the struggle to conform for reasons of safety and acceptance but feel stuck in a straitjacket. Our souls suffer. We either rebel or withdraw, but we still don't get to be ourselves. Goldenrod essence brings us the courage to be who we are and strengthens our personal power. This remedy works wonderfully on the rebellious teen who doesn't know what he or she wants but defiantly doesn't want it from you. The blessing of goldenrod essence is that it helps us identify the distinct sense of ourselves as individuals. We are strong enough to stand on our own convictions. The group mind no longer dictates who we are and what we believe. We are enough, and we have our own visions and dreams.

Goldenrod essence is best used when our individual choices may conflict with the choices of the group. We all want to belong. It is an important part of how we connect with others. Goldenrod essence works by helping us to grow into higher versions of ourselves. This essence supports us as individuals in coping with the pressures of how we should be and what we should do as dictated by those who know more. Goldenrod essence is the "I know and I choose" essence. "It is my turn to be me" — and that counts!

Goldenrod is also used when we don't feel the value for our stand-alone abilities. At these times, we may feel our value only as part of a family or organization or group. We smother our values, wants, and needs for the group's values, wants, and needs. When there is a great fear in us of standing alone or standing up for the simplest things we hold dear, goldenrod essence can help. It reminds us that the group's cohesiveness and powers come from the sum and value of its individual contributors. The more we retain and expand our personal values, the more all will benefit from our worth in what we have to offer. Our value begins with being the best we can be.

Golden Yarrow

Golden yarrow essence allows genuine expression. Many of us don't feel comfortable enough to be ourselves, especially if we are sensitive. We may mold ourselves to others' expectations of how we should be. We may find ourselves performing to various archetypes rather than performing as our authentic selves. Golden yarrow essence acts to strengthen our abilities to be authentic and sensi-

Quick Reference

- Eases impressionable tendencies
- Increases authenticity
- Makes it safe to be sensitive
- Encourages creativity

tive, allowing us to be more connected to our gifts and talents. It moves us from living in the shadow of our personal and creative expression to cocreating with all the tools available. Golden yarrow essence frees us to be protected while being ourselves.

Golden yarrow is sometimes referred to as the superman essence. It protects us from the energies of others. It helps those of us who have increased sensitivity and creative abilities feel safe and secure enough to access our gifts. Golden yarrow essence shows us how to fully express our vulnerability from a position of strength. It is a common remedy for actors, artists, and performers. It helps us to navigate that tightrope between being vulnerable enough to fully express ourselves but protected enough not to feel exposed. Golden yarrow essence is kryptonite for vulnerability and doubt. It helps us feel safe enough to be authentic and fully expressed.

Heather

Heather essence helps those people who feel that all their friends exist to pay them homage. They go on and on about every little detail of their lives and won't let anyone else get a word in. We all have friends like this — lively, talkative, and often entertaining. However, there is no exchange. These people require an audience, and when they don't have one, they may demand attention in some negative manner. It is their primary directive to be the focus of all attention. Heather essence helps to balance out this unabashed need. It can be used for either a temporary state — like an inability to stop talking about a recent trauma or drama — or a long-term state, such as a deep need to constantly legitimize one's pain.

Quick Reference

- Balances need for attention
- Helps with difficulty listening
- Creates empathy
- Provides emotional self-sufficiency

Thus, this essence is sometimes regarded as the motor mouth essence. We know we are in the presence of someone who needs heather when we feel all the life has been sucked out of the room. Think about heather as the "I want it all now" essence. When using heather, we no longer have to occupy space and time with incessant words. We begin to feel it is enough to be ourselves and to be willing to share words and ideas.

Heather

Heather isn't so much an essence for selfishness as it is for filling the void for loneliness, for when we don't feel real unless we are holding court with all of our concerns, dramas, and turmoil. With heather essence, the teenager in us can finally let someone else have a turn. It helps by allowing us to listen. It blesses us by helping others to be heard and feel at ease.

This remedy also assists in creating empathy. Heather balances the need to be heard with the desire to listen. It works by guiding us to an inner peace where words have value and the way we choose to express them is mindful rather than mindless. Heather essence provides emotional self-sufficiency. We no longer feel the compulsion to use words to fill up the lonely places. Our words have value, direction, and substance. Our words now create the desired effect.

Honeysuckle

Quick Reference

- Releases the old to make room for the new
- Breaks old cycles
- Engages the present
- Releases regrets, disappointments
- Opens the heart

Honeysuckle essence is the "stuck in the past" essence. Sometimes we feel life used to be so much better when we were with a certain person or we had a job, or we attended school. We get caught up in constantly comparing what happened in the "good old days" to the disappointment in the present. It is the essence for regrets. These can be simple regrets of a path not taken or profound regrets of a life not lived. Honeysuckle essence clears the emotional space held hostage by the past. It opens the heart and energy fields to be fully engaged with the gift of the present.

Honeysuckle helps remind us that everything happens for a reason. Whether we believe in soul growth or changing our energy vibration to correct our romantic actions from the past, honeysuckle essence helps us to work on being present. It provides us with the gift of ourselves and being in line with the right time. Honeysuckle stops us from slipping away. It makes us ready, willing, and able to be present with our presence.

This essence is used specifically for lack of inner movement. Our current resources will be limited if we're still reading yesterday's news. We are no longer defined by who we were; instead, we become who we are and who we want to be. This remedy helps us to fully engage in who we are and what we are doing and how the world holds promise for us. Some say honeysuckle makes them feel as if they are coming out of a dream and they are now ready for the world.

Honeysuckle essence also has many healing and cleansing applications. It can be used for young people leaving home for the first time as well as for changing residences. This essence is useful in cleansing and detoxification regimens, as it helps us to release the old so that we can make room for the new. It integrates our energy into new life choices. Honeysuckle essence is a positive tool for past-life regressions as well.

We expend so much vitality to live in two states of mind — where we were and where we are — that all of our present dreams vaporize due to lack of interest and energy. We may not have seen it at the time, but we wouldn't be here if we hadn't made the choices we made. When we use honeysuckle, we can clearly see how our choices have taken root in new abilities and new contracts for personal growth. Honeysuckle essence frees us from our emotional investment in keeping the past alive. We are able to use the past as a living foundation for the future. Old cycles are broken as we become present.

Hound's Tongue

Hound's tongue essence is for thinking "inside" the box. It's for those times when we know all the elements, but we don't see the magic. We see only what is in the most basic way. We are familiar with the box, and we know what is inside. We see four walls but not a world. We see cardboard but not what it will be used for. Hound's tongue teaches us to see our world in a new way. It teaches us to

Quick Reference

- Stimulates creative thinking
- Restores wonder
- Opens to new perspectives
- Incites imagination

think by seeing all of the possibilities of the imagination. It incites the active imagination by casting a whole other level of reality.

Hound's-tongue essence also helps with the "is that all there is?" mentality. We often get stuck in what we know and what we think we know. We find it difficult to step outside of the norm. Oftentimes, we see and perceive things as objects and functions. We pay more attention to what we think is going on rather than sensing the poetry of how it all connects. We might feel heaviness due to the limitations of the mundane. Hound's-tongue essence aids us by showing us the other side of the box. With its help, we can see the box's function and the structure of its dimensions, but we can also take the leap to see what it can carry and hold. There is a new energy that changes what we think we know. We feel our thought processes become lighter and more enlivened.

Indian Pink

Quick Reference

- Imbues composure
- Helps us remain centered
- Stills internal chaos
- Finds grace under pressure

Indian pink essence is used for the times when we are overwhelmed with the present, the times when there are too many details to attend to and not enough time. This is the essence for that spinning out of control feeling, of not being able to get a grip. Indian pink essence repairs the energy body, which can be torn or disturbed by too much emotional and psychic activity. Sometimes we feel as if we are in a centrifuge and all of our forces are being disturbed and distorted by too

Indian Pink

many demands. Indian pink essence helps us to manage and coordinate our lives by remaining centered.

I also like to think of Indian pink as the "running around like a chicken with its head cut off" essence. Some of us thrive in chaos, but most of us do not. The need for this essence reminds me of the episode of *I Love Lucy* when Lucy and Ethel were working at the candy factory on the conveyer belt. At first, they could handle the pace and were happy, laughing, and feeling a sense of accomplishment. Then the conveyer belt continued to speed up, and they became more and more stressed until they couldn't keep up and were stuffing pieces of candy into their mouths. I feel this is the point where many of us live — where we can't keep up anymore.

Sometimes we feel as if there are too many things to do in too little time. There are many conflicting demands that can leave us frazzled and frustrated. We feel like we can't stop and we can't differentiate. Indian pink is the essence for the times when we feel we need to be doing and moving in order to feel alive. When we define our life forces by how much we can achieve in any given time, Indian pink calms the agitation and reminds us of the strength of having a core of calm. Indian pink essence opens the window to being calm, cool, and collected.

Lady's Slipper

Quick Reference

- Aligns sense of purpose
- Connects to inner authority
- Integrates spiritual and physical energy
- Helps realize power

Lady's slipper essence is used when we work and work but don't feel a sense of purpose. We often find ourselves working just to work, and we get no sense of accomplishment from our jobs. Lady's slipper helps us to spiritually align with our purpose. It doesn't matter what we do but how we feel we are serving in the moment with all that we do. Lady's slipper essence is for walking our paths.

So much of the time, we can get stuck in our heads about what, how, when, and where we should be in life. Lady's slipper helps us to remember our connections to the greater good. We ultimately serve by being true to ourselves in our greatest expressions. Lady's slipper shows us how to walk in our power.

Lady's slipper is used when we feel cut off from our inner authority. At these times, we feel we are operating in some kind of limited capacity without integrating all of our talents through all of our chakras. It is as if we are using only a small percentage of what we have available. We function fully instead of having that sensation of being divided into two halves. This essence is a tonic for the nervous system. It eats away all the ambient electrical energy and channels it back into our overall health and welfare. It gives all we are and all we do more substance. Lady's slipper essence breaks the cycle of inertia; it gives us new direction.

Lavender

Lavender essence is used for nervous depletion. It calms nervous energy when we become consumed and exhausted. When we can't sit still or we can't get comfortable in our skin, lavender essence can soothe the nerves. It counteracts the effects of absorbing too much spiritual or mental energy. Lavender essence is also the essence for overstimulation. It helps you by dialing down your response to tensions. Lavender essence is particularly suited for highly sensitive people. It makes their sensitivity work for them rather than against them. It balances out the physical and nervous systems by soothing overresponsiveness and agitation.

Quick Reference

- Soothes nerves
- Helps the high strung
- Processes nervous energy
- Relieves tension
- Helps to "wind down"

Lavender essence sedates and calms the senses and nerves. It helps us pay attention to what needs attention as opposed to what we think needs attention. Lavender soothes the soul. With all the chaos, constant input, and sense of powerlessness that we experience in our daily lives, we don't know if we are coming or going. We can become so wound up that we don't know what to do with ourselves or how to channel the excess energy, and we end up vibrating with nervous tension. We can't let it go, and we feel all this pent-up energy trapped in our bodies. Lavender essence acts as a filter for all the energies that continue to stream into our consciousness. This essence helps us to release and moderate how we use our energy. We rebalance our emotional resources so we can fine-tune what we need and how we can be of true service.

Lavender

Lemon

Lemon is a cleanser and refresher. It cleans and clears our mental palate to energetically lighten our moods and thoughts, brightening our mental capacities and creative forces. This essence helps us to start off fresh, clearing any and all mental congestion.

The lemon plant is loaded with naturally occurring lithium that can stabilize our moods. It dissolves emotional scar tissue, lending calmness and coherence to emotions. Additionally, it softens the tendency to intellectualize emotions.

It's also helpful for those with attention deficit disorder (ADD) and lack of focus. Lemon is a great essence for students and anyone working through a prolonged study period, as it helps us retain and integrate new information. It also counteracts mental and intellectual laziness and clears mental blocks to learning new information, such as new algebra problems or upgraded software. Lemon works well for learning curves and instills confidence in our intellectual processes.

Quick Reference

- Refreshes the mind
- Increases clarity
- Helps ADD
- Balances creativity, intellect
- Eases mental exhaustion

Mimulus

Mimulus

Mimulus essence is used when fear casts a cloud over our daily lives. When we are afraid of the dark, afraid of earthquakes, or afraid that our neighbors might see us in our SpongeBob pajamas, we are letting fear get the best of our judgment. We find it limits us in the most mundane manner. We might find ourselves feeding the fear or even bargaining with it. Mimulus essence doesn't eliminate the fear per se, but it gives us the courage to face it head on.

Quick Reference

- Brings daily courage
- Manages fear
- Helps inner tension
- Aids in living with sensitivity

We feel the fear, and we act anyway. And as we face our fear, it generally dissolves or becomes manageable, more like an early warning system than a monster under the bed. Mimulus creates and cleanses by freeing us from the burden of fear and opening up our energy to courage and vitality.

Morning Glory

> **Quick Reference**
> - Eases hangovers
> - Helps erratic patterns
> - Tunes energy levels
> - Resets personal clock
> - Gives a fresh start

Morning glory essence wakes up our lives, giving us a fresh start. This essence is for those times when we might be going down undesirable paths or exhibiting nasty habits and we do not know how to break out of these cycles. We may be stuck in a rut or feel our natural light and vitality dim. This essence helps us feel the play between the light and the dark so that we can choose more light.

Morning glory essence turns the switch back on. It strengthens the etheric body, which in turn allows more life force to enter our bodies. It helps us become more in touch with the natural ebbs and flows of our energy fields. Thus we become more discerning about how our bodies use their resources. This is a great essence to start off the new year, as it works especially well for that hungover feeling.

Using this essence allows us to choose to direct energy for positive change. It helps those of us who are stuck in destructive patterns. This essence wakes us from our drug or habit of choice. It helps us to listen to the impulses and needs of the body. It resets our energy from the feeling of being drugged or dragged around back to natural vibrancy. We begin to feel our energy as our birthright. This is what it is like to feel good! Morning glory essence restores the innocence and radiance of the body. It harnesses the power of transitioning from dull to dynamic.

Morning Glory

Mountain Pennyroyal

Mountain Pennyroyal

Quick Reference

- Clears energy bodies
- Clarifies thinking
- Instills positivity
- Heals thoughts, reactions
- Helps psychic contamination

Mountain pennyroyal is the essence used for toxic thoughts and the absorption of the negative energies of others. Sometimes we can lose insight as to what energy is ours and what is from others. All we know is that all of a sudden, we feel "slimed," as the Ghostbusters say. This is one of those remedies for protection against ethereal entities and thought forms. It is the remedy for energy hygiene. Mountain pennyroyal clears stuck mental and emotional patterns, purging away toxic thoughts and feelings, creating a natural filter so our energy bodies are more our own. We cleanse and create by having clearer substance to work with.

When our sensitivity can cause us to absorb the not-so-pleasant effects of others, it becomes difficult to discern what belongs to us and what belongs to them. Have you ever been in a situation in which you were feeling fine, life was good, and you generally had no complaints, but then you went to a party or walked into a room and all of a sudden you felt sad, mad, or agitated? As we become more sensitive to energies, we are also sensitive to the broader spectrum of energy — both positive and negative. Mountain pennyroyal essence works by strengthening and clearing the mental body. It eliminates the chaotic and toxic mental debris. It systematically goes through and discards the energies that are not working for our greatest and highest good.

This essence helps us to clarify our thinking and eliminates psychic contamination. It clears toxic thought forms to prevent them from taking hold in the etheric body. Mountain pennyroyal makes us mindful of what thoughts are coming in and how we process them. It also helps us sort out the mental chaos and fight the energetic hijackers. It balances our energy fields and enhances our immune systems. When using it, we begin to feel a new clarity and appreciation for how our thoughts can inspire confidence rather than incite fear. Mountain pennyroyal works by healing our thoughts and our reactions to them.

Mustard

Quick Reference

- Combats doom and gloom
- Clears clouded consciousness
- Eases mood swings
- Fights hidden depression

When it feels as if the sky is literally falling, mustard essence helps to let the light back in. It brings forth hope and radiance. It works well when we feel depressed and off balance. Mustard essence is specific for heaviness of thinking and feeling. Traditionally, it's used for the type of depression that comes and goes — for those times when we feel fine, bright, and cheerful one moment but then turn into a deep, dark, depressed mess the next moment. We might not know where it came from or how it got there, but we feel burdened by the energy of the dark cloud that prevents any light from coming through.

Mustard

Mustard essence helps those dark clouds lift. It has a lightening and brightening effect. It combats the gloom and doom aspect. We feel ourselves transform, and we have the ability to let the sun shine inward. It is the perfect essence for the holiday blues. It stops us from going into the deep, dark pits of despair. Mustard essence also helps when we get a cold or flu — illnesses that tend to affect emotions — making us feel sad and hopeless, as if we will never get better. Mustard essence brightens the blues away.

Olive

Olive essence treats the utter fatigue of body and soul. It is primarily used for restoring recuperative powers after a period of extreme physical exhaustion. It kick-starts our healing powers. Olive essence works its miracles when we feel our energy is beat down into the ground and there is nothing more we can give. This essence is great for getting our mojo back. Olive essence is indicated for any healing crisis in which we have to draw on deep resources. It makes us listen to what our bodies and souls are telling us.

Quick Reference

- Relieves exhaustion
- Kick-starts healing powers
- Taps inner reserves
- Conserves strength

Pine

> **Quick Reference**
> - Liberates from unnecessary guilt
> - Balances responsibility
> - Brings perspective to the past

Pine essence is known as the guilt essence. It can help us with feelings of deep guilt and in times when we feel responsible for everything. It works when we become consumed with the darkness of our thoughts and deeds. It's for the times when we can feel our life forces oppressed by the weight of our choices. It's for the times we view our actions under a microscope and all our perceived misdeeds are amplified: We did it, we were wrong, and everything negative or bad that happens to us or anyone around us seems to be our fault. Pine essence helps us to liberate ourselves from unnecessary guilt. It helps us to look in the right direction or achieve an accurate vision of who we are and what we have accomplished in our lives. Pine essence frees us to be worthy of love and self-respect.

It can be exhausting to feel like everything is our fault. Pine essence instructs us to weigh out what is our responsibility and what is others'. We are not meant to be the depository of all that goes wrong around us. Pine frees us to be ourselves, warts and all. We forgive ourselves so that we can receive the blessings due to us and realize our true worth. It resets our ability to deserve. We learn that there are limits to our responsibility and that we become enough by not having to be enough for everyone else.

Sometimes we feel frozen in time as if we can't seem to move beyond a certain incident or expectation. When we dwell on past mistakes and failures, refusing to allow for the learning curve, forever stuck in "shoulda, coulda, woulda," pine essence brings perspective to our experiences. It allows us to learn that we all have contracts that we are here to live out as we learn through making certain choices and fulfilling our destinies. It gives us an overview — the ability to look at the big picture. We might not be able to do it in the moment, but eventually we can see what was served by the choices we did or didn't make.

If you find that you are saying sorry for everything, consider using this essence. It will give you your life back. The serenity prayer is the perfect prayer for the pine type: "God grant me the serenity to accept the things I cannot change, courage to change the things I can, and wisdom to know the difference" [Reinhold Niebuhr, 1892–1971].

Red Clover

Quick Reference

- Prevents mass hysteria
- Restores calm presence
- Finds personal equilibrium
- Realigns with self-wisdom

Red clover essence helps to prevent us from feeding into mass hysteria. Whether we are in a crowd or watching the news and reacting to all the current events, we can get caught in the tone or emotional turmoil of the crowd. We can become infected by the virus of thought through mass consciousness. Red clover essence helps to center and ground us so that we limit the effects of getting caught in tidal waves of emotion.

News headlines and the way they affect everyone around us can easily cause us to lose our personal equilibrium. The key here is to protect ourselves from being carried away by the group mind. Red clover is a powerful emotional balancer and cleanser. It helps us to extricate from the feeding frenzy of the group and to become calm and self-aware. It helps to remind us of who we are in the group: We are not the group; we are a part of the group. Red clover helps us to differentiate between the two. The more we have an active center, the more we can make choices and decisions that will come from calm strength as opposed to hysterical flux. We can make our decisions based on peace for the greatest good, not what is coming from the most fear.

This remedy restores our natural leadership and is an effective emotional cleanser. It clears the effects of media images and mass negativity. It helps us to realign with the wisdom of the self rather than the tidal wave of the group. Red clover essence helps us to create the change by being aware of how we choose to participate in change.

Rockrose

Rockrose is the essence we use to alleviate the panic that comes from either experiencing or feeling the fear of a worst-case scenario. This remedy is an integral component of the Rescue Remedy formula (see Special Combinations chapter). It is traditionally used for those who feel as if they're being immobilized by fear or terror. Rockrose reminds us that we have courage, helping us to face our fears. With its assistance, we do whatever we need to do — any way and any how. It doesn't eliminate the fear, but it gives us the tools to confront fear-based limitations.

Quick Reference

- Alleviates panic
- Mobilizes against fear
- Musters courage
- Puts fear in perspective
- Accesses internal guidance

Rationally, this essence is used for phobias that can be extremely limiting. However, it can also be used when we can't seem to move forward or backward — when we feel stuck and scared and can't take the next step. Rockrose essence unfreezes us. We can still be scared and stifled by our emotions but move forward anyway. This remedy lends peace and tranquility to our challenges and helps us to put them in perspective. Rockrose allows us to mobilize our forces.

Rockrose essence is also used for those times when we lose perspective because our reactions are over the top. It's helpful when we feel that we won't survive and all of our physical reactions escalate until we almost shut down. Rockrose essence restores our ability to react and respond appropriately. We access what we need in order to muster the courage required. This remedy gives us access to our internal guidance.

Sage

Quick Reference

- Reveals life's worth
- Accesses wisdom
- Processes life experiences
- Eases life transitions

Sage essence addresses the trials and tribulations of our lives. When we begin to focus on our missteps — what we didn't do as opposed to what we did do — sage essence gives us perspective. There is elegance to this essence. It has a way of energetically revealing to us the worth of our lives, and it lends us a sense of peace and accomplishment. Sage essence can help us to see our sacred contracts and to make peace with them. It provides the necessary elevation to show that we are all important and that we all serve in our own ways.

This essence helps us to process our experiences in such a way that we can extract the wisdom and meaning. It helps us to access the sage within. It can help filter and distill what experiences have and haven't worked. It lends emotional validity to what we know and makes us more accepting of our individual realities.

Sage essence can help us to have more of an appreciation for the journey without discounting the stumbling and fumbling along the way.

It illuminates the value of the entire experience — not just the good parts. It helps us to see with clarity how all points do truly lead to now. It helps us to bypass some of the regrets by shifting our perception. It lends grace and compassion for the walk, not the destination. Sage essence is an excellent remedy for life-review work or whenever there is a huge transition that we just can't seem to make sense of.

Sagebrush

Sagebrush essence breaks through the images we create for ourselves. We may be attached to our money, our positions, or our roles as extensions of how we define or characterize ourselves. We become so attached to the veneer that we lose our soul connection. Sagebrush reconnects us to all of our parts and makes a soul "correction." We are no longer defined by what we do or how much we have but by who we are.

Quick Reference

- Refines self-image
- Helps rebirth
- Removes past conditioning
- Frees from illusion
- Aids in personal evolution

Sagebrush helps us to look in the mirror and see who we are. We are soul expressions as well as more than the sum of our parts and experiences. Using sagebrush helps us experience ourselves as culminations of love and light. We vibrate and resonate through all of our selves. We naturally integrate and become more in touch with who we are, not what we do. This essence removes our past conditioning. This is an excellent midlife crisis formula. We can become too attached to our personal histories and become ingrained in how we interpret ourselves. Sagebrush essence offers rebirth. It helps by moving us forward into our destinies. This essence frees us from what no longer works for us. We come face to face with our core selves and core issues. Sagebrush essence allows us to change through inner freedom and taking the next step.

We often have an inkling of what we need, but we become afraid that we have something to lose: Who will we become, and how will that look? In many ways, sagebrush is an essence for our current times. It helps us to find ourselves. It helps us to evolve. It fortifies us in the struggle to become. Sagebrush essence aids in our personal transformation — the transformation of the mock-up version of ourselves into our real substance. With the help of this essence, we can make sense of our personal existence without having to justify ourselves in material terms. It helps us to see, feel, and create the magic of ourselves.

Sagebrush aids us in dissolving the props so we can access who we really are. This essence works when we come to the point in our lives when we begin to question the values we have held and the contributions we have made. We question what we have invested our time in and what meaning these things continue to hold. Does the perceived value have a hold over us, or do we have a hold over it? This is a "take stock" formula: with its help, we can take stock of who and what we are and what we have become. Our value comes from the ability to look in the mirror — warts and all — and respect the journey.

Sagebrush

Scleranthus

> **Quick Reference**
> - Helps make choices
> - Gives strength, substance to decisions
> - Eases inner restlessness
> - Fosters trust in personal judgment

Scleranthus essence is the "should I do this or should I do that?" essence. It is used for the times when we cannot make up our minds or when each decision we need to make feels life changing. This essence helps us figure out how to make those decisions. Many of us become paralyzed by the belief that if we make one decision, it will lock us into a process and block access to other possibilities. Scleranthus essence helps us with the concept of making a decision a better way. Decisions open doorways. One decision will lead to another rather than forever limiting us to a single track.

This essence encourages belief in the process of forward movement. It is an essence of faith. Scleranthus reminds us that no matter how stuck we are, movement will provide its own safety net. It helps us learn to leap. It balances us so that we don't feel locked in by our choices.

Scleranthus is sometimes regarded as the crossroads formula. It provides guidance when we feel confusion and experience anxiety about which path to take. When there is a sense of feeling trapped by the choices we are faced with, scleranthus essence helps us with that fidgety quality — the feeling of not getting it right. It calms us by helping us trust ourselves and our instincts. We feel at peace, not trapped.

Oftentimes, we can't focus, and we flit from one thing to another. Then we miss opportunities because we can't make up our minds, and as a result, we fret over what more we could have done. Scleranthus essence helps us by giving strength and substance to our decisions. It provides the road to the next step, and we are able to create passages of progress. It helps us feel new possibilities, making us surer in our steps. We become flexible in our thinking. We find our internal balance and learn to trust ourselves. We become deciders.

Scleranthus essence encourages us to trust in our personal judgment. We trust that we can see and feel the differences between the choices we face. We no longer feel stymied and trapped by the fear of making the wrong decision. Instead, we feel the element of guidance and working with what is appropriate for us. Our choices begin to make more sense to our sensibilities, and we feel empowered by the necessary changes rather than anxious.

How many times have we done nothing because we were afraid to do something? With scleranthus's influence, we are no longer stymied by the decisions we face. We feel the prospects and have more confidence. Scleranthus essence helps us to look at the bigger picture. It encourages us to exercise our ability to make a choice and follow through, giving us the ability to adjust or choose differently as new circumstances arise.

Self-Heal

Quick Reference

- Activates healing
- Restores wholeness
- Promotes wellness
- Counteracts overdependence
- Restores belief

Self-heal essence is one of the components of the Yarrow Special Formula. The essence of the self-heal plant does exactly what its name says it does. Self-heal remedy enhances all of our healing energies. It is invigorating and stimulating, and it rallies our healing forces. I like working with this essence, as it helps to flip the switch over to health. When we have been feeling discouraged about health issues, it helps us take responsibility for our own recovery. It helps us to trust in what we need for our recovery and to break away from the dogma of how we are "supposed" to mend.

Often we feel we need something or someone other than ourselves to help us recover after an injury or illness. Sometimes we feel we have lost the capacity to believe we can be well or whole again. We no longer know how to take responsibility for ourselves and our healing processes.

Self-heal essence inspires us to tap into our healing reserves. It works well for those times when we lose faith or trust in the body's abilities to heal and do what comes naturally. We forget what we have and how to use it. This essence reminds us that we have what we need at any given time. It helps us fight for what is right for our health and healing processes.

Think about this essence as an energy salve to fill in or weave together etheric pieces that have been ripped, shredded, torn, or damaged by any number of issues or illnesses. Self-heal essence helps us to work toward our personal wholeness. It custom tailors its healing properties toward what we need to rejuvenate. If we need more faith to heal by remembering how to be well or if we need to tap into the bigger picture of our healing challenges, this essence delivers.

Self-heal essence shows us how to pay attention to the clues to health and healing and what it feels like to be whole again. It activates our innate healing abilities. We can use it as an individual essence or to augment other essences, supplementing their healing effects. Self-heal essence works on the etheric and emotional bodies. It repairs the energetic sheaths in order to restore the integrity of the energy fields. It alleviates doubt by shifting awareness from negativity to confidence, which restores hope. Self-heal helps remind us how to take the first step to move beyond emotional and physical stagnation.

Star of Bethlehem

Star of Bethlehem is one of the components in the Rescue Remedy formula (see Special Combinations chapter). It is used for the direct effects of shock. It helps to neutralize the trauma and restore our equilibrium. We get through the worst of it and move forward but oftentimes feel limited by the experience. It is as if we get stuck in a certain gear. For the most part, we are functioning in our lives, but we cannot seem to get over some particular event. It can be a big event such as Hurricane Katrina or a small incident such as the wrong word said at the wrong time.

Quick Reference

- Neutralizes trauma
- Restores equilibrium
- Provides comfort
- Gives freedom and energy to move forward

Star of Bethlehem works by neutralizing the trauma. It has a way of doing a spiritual chiropractic adjustment. It helps release old, trapped traumas — both physical and emotional — and aligns us with the highest versions of ourselves. Unencumbered by the past, we are no longer limited by what has happened to us. Star of Bethlehem gives us the freedom and energy to begin again and move forward.

Star of Bethlehem

St. Johnswort

Quick Reference

- Helps utilize our light
- Protects lightbodies, energy fields
- Balances light sensitivity

St. Johnswort is for those of us who are very sensitive and overly expanded. It offers protection when we are feeling "way out there." This essence has a positive centering and grounding effect. It helps us to work with our light in a more powerful way. Many of us are affected by too little light and suffer from seasonal affective disorder (SAD), for example, which lowers our vitality. Many of us are also affected by too much light and heat. Think about how you might feel drained by too much sunshine after a day at the beach.

This essence helps us utilize our light. We feel the light within illuminating who we are. We feel the vibration of the light acting as a natural shield to negative elements, whether these come through dreams or from astral travel. This essence gives our personal fields more integrity. It allows us to feel the illumination and warmth of the light without getting lost in overly expanded awareness.

St. Johnswort is a great protective essence. It is restorative, allowing us to root expanded awareness and to balance sensitivity. When using this essence, we can feel the effects of the light of awareness becoming integrated into our everyday lives. We feel the strength of our light within. We feel more connected to the spiritual forces available. When we do not have proper rooting in our spiritual practices, we can become blinded by the light and lose the connection to ourselves. St. Johnswort protects our lightbodies and helps us to circulate our light in a grounded and empowered way. It protects our energy fields from energetic distortion and also strengthens, restores, and protects our subtle bodies.

Tiger-Lily

Quick Reference

- Helps menopause
- Relaxes aggressive tendencies
- Lessens harsh competition
- Helps cooperation
- Balances gender

Tiger-lily essence is especially helpful for women who feel that they have to be a beast — or the B word — in order to be seen and heard. It is for those among us demonstrating the screaming meemies. There are times when we may feel that we have to be the strongest, yell the loudest, be the best, be the most competent, do the most work, and be the most visible. We also feel exhausted and misunderstood by the way we are trying to get everyone onboard. Tiger-lily promotes the positive feminine expression of leadership. The power comes from cooperation and a stepping down of the yang-style energy.

I love the way it helps by working "for" rather than "against." We feel more comfortable expressing our version of leadership rather than the dictates of what a leader is supposed to look like. Tiger-lily essence allows us to feel more inclusive, especially of ourselves. It allows us to feel the shift from high-wire competition to high-wire cooperation.

Tiger-Lily

Trillium

Quick Reference

- Overcomes greed
- Builds self-esteem
- Increases self-worth
- Shifts motivation from power to service

Trillium essence helps us during those times when our motivation is purely for power and material goods. It's for the times when we always want more. The feeling doesn't go away, and we never feel the pleasure of the result. It's as if there is a deep, black hole that can only be filled with what we can get, but we never get there. Trillium essence helps to balance this primary motivation for power and "stuff." It fills the need by helping us shift from the single-minded pursuit of power to the pursuit of service through our abilities.

With the help of this essence, we are no longer so self-obsessed with what we "want, want, want for me, me, me." Our drive becomes the vehicle for achievement and connection. Our focus becomes balanced, true motivation along with the sense of completion and a job well done.

Vine

Quick Reference

- Increases respect for others
- Fosters true leadership
- Promotes service
- Refines natural authority

Vine essence is for the know-it-all control freak — or for dealing with the know-it-all control freak. It is for those times when we have to have it our way, when we feel that we know better than anyone and won't take no for an answer. Sometimes we become relentless in our pursuit of what we think is right. It is our way or the highway. When we assume our natural leadership with the

utmost authority, vine flower remedy helps us to back down. It softens the iron hand of how things should be.

This essence is also quite effective for those of us who need to have the last word. It helps release the tension. It breaks the pattern of always having to add one more thing. Peace comes with the knowledge of leading by example and being the people we ourselves would look up to. It helps us to lead in the way we would like to be led.

White Chestnut

White chestnut essence is indicated for those times when we can't let go of mindless brain chatter. This is the remedy specifically for all our feelings of "shoulda, coulda, woulda." It is a perfect antidote when we find ourselves constantly and consistently ruminating over what we need to do, what we should have done, and what we think we should do. White chestnut essence interrupts the rumination process. It interferes with that hamster wheel our minds sometimes like to run in circles on.

Quick Reference

- Provides peace
- Eases mind chatter
- Helps concentration
- Releases tension in head, jaw

How many times have we lain in bed, trying to get some sleep but instead obsessed over what we should have done or what we could have said better, deciding what we will do to fix it, and pondering why we always get ourselves into these sorts of messes? White chestnut remedy calms the mind and helps us to discern what we need to pay attention to and what we don't.

This remedy gives us an off switch. It imbues us with clarity and focus, letting us sort out our thoughts and reprioritize our tasks. It relaxes our brains and allows our thoughts to flow and form new creative solutions. White chestnut essence releases obsessive thoughts and locates the missing inspired action. This essence provides an integrative approach to personal harmony. It stops the cerebral CD from skipping without having to discard it. We can now think ourselves out of the box.

White chestnut is a mental clearing essence. As this essence takes effect, thoughts no longer have runaway lives of their own, and we feel more mastery over our powers of concentration. When the constant white noise or chatter is quelled, we can use our mental powers for more productive uses. White chestnut essence has the added benefit of releasing tension in the head and jaw and thus is also a remedy for teeth grinding. It relieves constant gnawing and unproductive energy drain.

White Chestnut

Wild Oat

Wild oat essence is a catalyst for growth. It is traditionally used for people who can do many things but master none — a jack-of-all-trades. It is different from some of the other indecision remedies, such as scleranthus. Wild oat essence is for those moments when we ask, "What is the choice or path I should take for my life?" "Where am I best served, and what are my real talents?" Wild oat clears the way. It gives direction.

Quick Reference

- Gives direction
- Works as a catalyst for growth
- Helps with prioritization
- Focuses life direction

This is a great remedy for when we can't decide what to do first. It has a prioritizing effect on what to do next, allowing us to feel movement and clarity. Wild oat allows us to create a unique sorting process so that we can rapidly decide what works for us and, more importantly, what doesn't work. Using this essence helps us to become more discerning. We start to pay attention only to those things that will help us to mine the true gold within.

Zinnia

Zinnia

Quick Reference

- Lends joy
- Gives permission to play
- Revives sense of humor
- Balances freedom and obligation

Zinnia essence reminds us to play and find joy. Joy and play are often removed from the equation of success and the ability to commit. However, much more creativity and possibility become available when we allow ourselves to play. We can play by ourselves or with other people. We can play just to feel a pure expression of joy. Zinnia essence brings out the essential ability to suspend the format of the intellect and allow for free-flowing freshness. Zinnia essence acts as a breath of fresh air to fight generalized boredom. It reminds us that God has a sense of humor and much is accomplished by the value of light and play.

We might think that treats and tricks are for kids, often taking our somber sense of adulthood as a destination on the road map of maturity. Sometimes we even make a declaration that "this is how it is" and dismiss the need for levity and light. Zinnia essence helps us delight in life. It can help us balance the need for responsibility with the need to soar. Zinnia inspires the sense of freedom that comes from starting fresh with no expectations. It opens us to experience life with a lighter heart and in a playful mode. It integrates the lightness and joy with obligation and our sense of duty.

Zinnia is an essence of spontaneity that dissolves stale patterns of reactivity and inertia. It activates our funny bones and natural sense of vitality. We can often become consumed with the requirements of adulthood and lose our sense of humor. Humor is a necessary component for overall happiness. We can become stuck and feel too serious, as this is our interpretation of what it means to be mature and responsible. We have come to realize that this concept is overrated and misleading. Zinnia essence restores a sense of lightness. It counteracts all the heavy feelings of "shoulda, coulda, woulda." It helps us to become present and playful and teaches us that laughter is a necessity for health, work, and creativity.

This is a great remedy when working with animals and children, as it creates communication through playful activities. Think about the last time you played with a puppy or a baby. Smiles, giggles, and general silliness are their natural state of being. Playing is necessary for soul growth. Did you ever notice how your real thoughts and feelings come to the surface when you are playing? This is a back door to the real you.

With all the work we do, it is that much more important to have and participate in play. Play can mean many things to many people. Zinnia essence brings forth the abilities to engage and play. Play leads to creativity and change as well as getting out of our own way. Zinnia essence is the anti-serious essence. It reminds us not to take ourselves so seriously at the expense of our life and brightness quotients.

CHAPTER TWO

Barrier Busters

Let us have a breakthrough instead of a breakdown. Let us trust ourselves and not be artificially held back by old patterns or old thought forms. Let us be free enough to free ourselves so we can all be free to be ourselves.

Arnica

Arnica

Arnica essence releases us from the effects of old patterns of trauma and drama. Sometimes we trap the emotional insults from the past in our bodies and do not realize that they are the source of myriad pains and strains. All we know is *that* headache doesn't go away or *that* shoulder pain started when we argued with our kids or *that* knee gives out every time we overdraw our accounts. Arnica essence unlocks recurrent patterns to liberate us, and it also helps us by integrating our past experiences.

Quick Reference

- Unlocks recurrent trauma
- Releases blocked patterns
- Frees energy
- Aids emotional recovery
- Restores vitality

The action of the energy of arnica essence is similar to pulling out a long, painful splinter that has been deeply embedded and covered with old scar tissue. It creates a new pathway to healing, breaking through limitations and unconscious patterns while healing the reverberations of old traumas.

By using arnica essence, our energy becomes integrated and the shock embedded in the energy system is released. This essence relaxes, releases, and allows us to flow again. Arnica stops the dissociation and empowers us with new associations. We maneuver through the aches and pains that defined us and move toward the freedom into the now. Its focus is on recovery from the process. As we unpeel the different layers, we feel ourselves becoming lighter and freer from the obstacles of the past. We no longer use unconsciousness as a protective coating. We feel the freedom of awareness and we feel free to be conscious.

I also like this essence for abrupt changes. Arnica essence helps us when we become shifted from daily awareness or when we feel as if our spirits are being torn from our bodies. Arnica essence helps to reunite our bodies. It soothes and eases. This essence is a great emotional recovery remedy. It can be used for short-term shock or old, deep-seated shock that has become trapped in the body. Arnica essence liberates, allowing us to feel more conscious and more in tune with how we choose to participate. It restores vitality and the zest for life.

Black Cohosh

Quick Reference

- Balances fear with strength
- Shatters illusions
- Confronts and breaks destructive patterns

Black cohosh essence is used for the times when we choose to be in the shadows due to negative relationships. It is good for situations in which the elements of fear or apprehension are preventing us from showing our true selves or moving forward, situations in which we may find ourselves retreating rather than confronting what is best for us. Black cohosh essence helps us to balance our fear with our strength.

Black Cohosh

The keyword with this essence is "confrontation." This doesn't mean we have to confront the bully before we are ready. This essence shows us how to access the internal resources that will allow us to stop hiding in fear, whether we are hiding from ourselves or from others. This essence is traditionally used for abusive situations, emotional entanglements, and their aftereffects. I choose to use it for creating breakthroughs out of emotional stagnation. It helps to release us from destructive and addictive patterns of behavior, whether they are emotional or physical. It is an essence for the dark, dreary, and destructive.

Black cohosh essence works by confronting old patterns from the past. This is very much a "breaking the cycle" essence. It helps us to utilize energies that have been channeled into a destructive cycle for our growth and healing. By confronting our abuses, addictions, and destructive patterns, we can make the necessary changes to interrupt old cycles. This essence helps us to meet those dark places within. Finally, we can move beyond our limitations and disrupt the magnetic pull to the lower energies. We are no longer trapped by ancestral patterns or station in life.

Black-Eyed Susan

Quick Reference

- Provides illumination
- Aids in soul retrieval
- Deepens insight into experience
- Restores wholeness

Black-eyed Susan essence is indicated for repressed fears. It is used for those of us who are hiding out from the scary parts of ourselves. We don't want to see them. This essence helps us to see and be ourselves safely. It increases the awareness of all aspects of our psyches and where those aspects want us to go. It bathes our fears and shadows with light — the light of truth, the light of awareness, the light of healing, and the light of insight. This essence teaches us the art of shadow play so that we are no longer fearful of what is hiding in our deep, dark recesses. We soon realize that there is knowledge to be gained by facing our fears.

The very act of suppressing or having missing pieces of what we remember or choose to deal with is a huge energy expenditure. When we use our insight and awareness, many of us feel a huge energy release and gain greater access to our available energy and creative forces. In other words, we have the energy to create, clear, and cooperate with all

Black-Eyed Susan

the aspects of ourselves. Black-eyed Susan essence helps us to clear the shadow so we can clear the fear.

Black-eyed Susan is also known as a soul retrieval essence. It helps us recover our missing soul fragments. We forget, we suppress, we invalidate, or we minimize, but we still have missing pieces striving for wholeness. Black-eyed Susan essence shows us how to let our light safely shine on all the hidden aspects of the past. This remedy supports the excavation of all our deep, dark choices. It deepens our insight into the hows and whys of our experiences. Black-eyed Susan essence transforms the pain of what happened then into the beauty and full expression of what we are now. It opens the door to ideas and issues that may control us without our realization. Our issues percolate up through the surface, and we are no longer limited to what we were.

This essence helps us to remember our convictions. It helps us to remember the parts of ourselves that make us who we are. It makes us aware of our power and our progress. Black-eyed Susan essence frees us from our pasts. It heals by bringing to light what may be holding us back. It transforms hidden and trapped energies and channels them into personal growth and insight.

Centaury

> **Quick Reference**
> - Helps with personal boundaries
> - Restores core sense of self
> - Encourages authentic expression
> - Knows when to say no

Centaury is sometimes regarded as the Cinderella formula because it works on the need to serve others at our own expense. It helps those of us who take whatever is dished out when we don't know how to stand our ground. Oftentimes, we go along with the program because we fear not pleasing others. It is for these types of situations that centaury is our fairy godmother dust! We don't have to be right, and we don't have to be wrong. Centaury helps us learn how to trust our version of what is right for us. We learn how to be of service to others through who we are, not who others want us to be.

This "get a grip" formula helps with personal boundaries. Examine the areas in your life where you need to say no and note how you feel when you do. Is it something that you avoid at all costs? Are you afraid of not being liked or of being regarded as bad, mean, or selfish? Do you feel like you don't know how to go after what you want? Or worse, do you feel that you will be faulted for having your own life and desires? Centaury essence is tailor-made to correct these issues.

Centaury essence restores our core sense of self. Under its influence, we no longer feel defined by how much we do. We begin to own our skills

Centaury

and abilities as well as the ways in which we contribute. This essence helps us realize that we are good enough just the way we are. It also helps us when we're striving to lose those last ten pounds, when we're trying to avoid that obnoxious argument at all costs, or when we are having a difficult time standing up for what we want and what we think is right.

Using centaury helps us feel the strength of who we are and begin to take our own wants and needs into consideration. It helps us see that it is okay to have boundaries and it is okay to exercise our values. It teaches us that being true to ourselves is our most authentic expression. Centaury also addresses allergies and irritations by reminding us that we all have autonomy and natural boundaries. This formula helps the body to stimulate its natural defense systems by just saying no.

Chestnut Bud

Quick Reference

- Helps learning
- Breaks limiting patterns
- Brings confidence to grow

Chestnut bud essence is for the times when we are stuck repeating the same old patterns. We gather all the advice we can from every resource until we have exhausted them and everyone around us, and we still can't decide what to do. So we start the whole process over again. It's as if we are stuck watching *Gone with the Wind* over and over, expecting Rhett Butler to give a damn.

Chestnut bud essence teaches us how to learn from our experiences. This is one of the pattern-breaker essences, as it illuminates the pitfalls so that we don't have to attract that lesson or that pattern again. Chestnut bud essence helps us evolve to change our responses. We should use this essence when we are stuck in a never-ending loop. We know what and how we want to do things. We know we need to change and very much want to, but here we are again, stuck in the same type of relationship or with the same extra twenty pounds or with the same evil, no-good boss. We forget that the common denominator is ourselves.

Strength and freedom come from breaking the cycle. We change our karma by changing our patterns, the way we participate in life, and how we make decisions. Chestnut bud essence increases the awareness of how our patterns might be working for us or — more importantly — against us. It shows us that we have to pay attention and that we learn more readily from observing the successes of others. This essence brings us confidence to allow our abilities to grow and thrive. It springs us forward by releasing us from old cycles of limitation.

This essence is also helpful when we have obsessive-compulsive tendencies. It can give us the peace to try something new. Chestnut bud essence shows us how to pay attention to the cues of a more empowered life. Those of us caught in any of these situations are in dire need of it. This essence breaks negative patterns, creating an energy shift that will assist us to gain greater perspective so that we can process experiences in a more progressive manner.

Dandelion

Quick Reference

- Relaxes tension
- Supports natural flow
- Promotes ease
- Helps us "unplug"
- Slows things down

Dandelion essence is the intensity remedy. It is for the times when we have been holding on very tightly, bracing for our future. Our internal tension may have been holding us together, but now it is fusing the energies of what we want with what we don't want. There is little separation and that much tension saps our energy. We use dandelion essence to release internal tension and to relax pent-up musculature from holding on too tightly or trying too hard. One of its more powerful uses is releasing cases of emotional rigidity. There is no flow. Dandelion essence supports natural flow.

This essence is also used for the tendency we sometimes have to "muscle" our way through our work. As we work to create our opportunities, we sometimes keep going until we can't stop. When we work and work and never get to where we think we need to go, the result is

toxic build-up of unfulfilled drives. This essence helps to alleviate that building internal tension. When the drive is there but we have forgotten the destination, dandelion essence breaks the cycle.

I believe this is the perfect essence for all the techies out there. We are on our phones, on our mobile devices, watching TV, checking email, and trying to fill every minute with the utmost efficiency. But then we don't know how to turn it all off. We might believe we are being effective; however, our innate tension to keep doing what we are doing exacts a toll on our energy levels. Thus, we never feel like we are doing enough.

Dandelion essence lets us focus our attention on releasing what no longer works for us. It helps to free us from the grip of the question, "What is going to happen next?" It allows us to breathe. Dandelion is an excellent remedy for slowing down our pace so that we can listen to what our bodies need, not what we need our bodies to do. This essence doesn't encourage sloth but allows us to utilize our energy more effectively and efficiently. Dandelion essence's gift is to instruct us to use the right amount of energy for the job and not trap our unrealized dreams in our bodies.

Hornbeam

Quick Reference

- Enhances vitality
- Relieves drudgery
- Refreshes attitude
- Restores enthusiasm
- Inspires new routines

Hornbeam is often regarded as the "Monday morning" essence. This is the remedy to use for being stuck in stark routines, such as performing any job we feel we can do by standing on our heads, when every day seems much like the one before it. During these times, hornbeam essence is our shot of emotional caffeine. It gives us a jolt when we are tired, bored, or in a rut. Hornbeam raises our energy levels.

This essence is also known as the "dreading it all" essence. It isn't used for dread as in danger but dread as in "here we go again." Hornbeam can help us in those times when our next step feels like just one more thing to do. Hornbeam essence injects vitality and mental creativity. It helps us to transform "I can't do it anymore" into "I can do it even better!" Hornbeam helps us to realize our potential in every circumstance. It helps us to manage our time and energy. It has the refreshing quality of tapping into unknown or unexplored resources within. Hornbeam reestablishes communication between where we are and where we are going, giving us the energy required for the task.

This remedy is a great pattern breaker for when we become too stuck in unsatisfying and unhealthy routines, such as overeating, overworking, or watching too much TV. Hornbeam helps shake things up when we work too much and we have been neglecting exercise, leaving us feeling stale and stuck. It helps us recognize and act on the need for balance.

Hornbeam essence rouses us when we feel exhausted before we even get started. It helps us bring on a sense of newness, inspiring the feeling we have when something new, exciting, or different comes our way. Hornbeam aids us by helping to provide a new vision or a sense of the new to our old and tired tasks and obligations. We reinvest in a more empowered way. We see what we have to do as a means to an end rather than "the end." Hornbeam helps us discover how to use energy in more effective manners. We learn how to balance routines and be open to variety.

Hornbeam

Oregon Grape

Oregon Grape

> **Quick Reference**
>
> - Eases paranoia
> - Fosters trust
> - Interrupts patterns
> - Releases protective anger

Oregon grape essence works for those times when we feel that everything is out to get us, when our perceptions read the worst in people instead of the best, and when we have a tendency to be paranoid and look for hidden agendas. If our version of reality is that no one can be trusted and we have to be constantly on the defensive, we feel excluded. We can feel these tendencies pop up in any situation in which we feel we have to be on guard. Oregon grape breaks down these barriers of mistrust. It shows us how to look for the good in others. It helps us to trust our own judgment so that we can trust others. When we trust ourselves and our own judgment, we become more protective, as we are following our inner cues of safety and protection.

Oregon grape essence is useful for those times when we expect anger and hostility from others. With this mindset, we can easily find ourselves in a negative feedback loop — expecting the worst from others and getting exactly what we expect. Sometimes we get paranoid, and we feel as if we have an aura of negativity around us. It can seem as if we can see what we are manifesting before our very eyes. We expect bad things, and so we get bad things; we expect anger, and so we get anger.

When we are in these states of instant negative manifestation, Oregon grape essence helps us to break that cycle. With its help, we easily change our patterns by seeing how we contribute to creating the patterns. We can step outside of ourselves and refresh our energy patterns. We no longer need our anger to protect us.

Willow

Willow essence is the ultimate essence for resentment and not feeling that we are getting our due. This is the essence to use when we are playing the blame game. We can't do what we want to do because someone or something is not letting us do it; thus, the cycle begins. Willow essence is also the perfect essence to use in treating grudges. Sometimes we find ourselves not doing the things we like and love as a reaction to some slight we have received. We use willow essence for the times when we seem to be cutting off our noses to spite our faces.

Quick Reference

- Releases resentment
- Overcomes bitterness
- Helps forgive, forget
- Provides positive influence
- Promotes cooperation

Willow

Willow essence allows us to see that we have a hand in our fate. This essence is the antidote for the victim mentality, and it allows us to get over ourselves and get on with our lives. Willow essence activates our faith and inner reserves. It shows us the bigger picture of how all points lead to the present for our purpose and growth. It relieves the itch by scratching the surface of old wounds and resentments. We are all familiar with the feeling of never getting what we want, no matter how hard we try. At times, we begrudge the accomplishments of others and feel we haven't gotten a fair shot.

This essence is sometimes known as the "blaming and shaming" essence — "blaming" that we feel life isn't fair and "shaming" because it is so hard to admit how we may have contributed. Willow essence has the ability to show us how to take responsibility. It helps us to respond more appropriately to life's lessons by giving an overview of how we have contributed to our own circumstances. It lightens us up and lets us see the bigger picture.

We should use willow for those times when we are struck because we feel someone or some circumstance is holding us back: We can't do "this" because of "that," which creates a lot of anger, bitterness, and stagnation. Willow helps us to release anger and resentments. We take whatever responsibility we can for moving forward in spite of all that has happened or all the obstacles that may exist. Using this essence has a liberating effect. With its help, we are no longer bound by our perceived limitations. We no longer play the blame game. Willow essence helps us to go with the flow. It removes the sense of being stuck. It changes us from "I can't, because _____!" to "Yes, I can!"

CHAPTER THREE

Divine Connection

Our purpose is simpler and more profound than we can possibly imagine. We have many guides to cheer us on along the way and many signs to keep us going in the right direction. Our primary focus is to be our best, to be generous in spirit, and to express compassion.

Angelica

> **Quick Reference**
> - Connects to divine guidance
> - Gives spiritual protection
> - Breaks isolation
> - Promotes angelic connection

Angelica essence is known as the "guardian angel" essence. Whenever we fear something, hold ourselves back, or feel as if we "can't," this essence reminds us that we can. Angelica acts to reconnect us with our guidance and our divinity. It helps us become aware of when we are cut off. We can become so overstressed and focused on what is not happening or what is going wrong that we can lose our connection to anything other than our problems and challenges. Angelica essence reminds us that we have a whole other world that can aid and assist us in untold ways. It frees us from the shadow and illusion that we are all alone.

This is a beautiful essence for feeling the guidance and access to our angels, guides, and God within. It helps us create a living relationship with the angelic realm. Angelica essence connects us to the divine within. It establishes a feeling vocabulary with our spiritual nature. Angelica essence has excellent protection properties. Primarily it helps to protect us from feeling cut off or disconnected from our source. It helps us to realize that we are part of something much bigger than ourselves. This essence almost whispers to us that guidance has always been available; all we ever had to do was ask. We feel a great sense of protection wash over us as we work with angelica. We feel more alive and more connected.

This essence has a way of making us feel that we are not alone, that our spiritual family is always with us.

Angelica essence is excellent for change and transitions. It lends us a layer of peace and acceptance, wherever we are. I like to think that it gives us breathing space by creating a sense of calm within, whatever storms are going on around us. It helps us to bridge the gap so that we don't feel so isolated and alone. We feel the support. It helps us to transcend our own limitations that arise out of the fear of the unknown.

Whether it is the birthing process, reconnection, or transitioning to the other side, angelica offers its magic through its innate sense of protection and feeling the love. We can never lose ourselves if we know we are connected to Source. It works great as a spiritual safety net. When we use it, we remember that we have backup. We remember that we have value in heaven's eyes.

Angel's Trumpet

Quick Reference

- Assists major transitions
- Helps in trusting change
- Surrenders to the unknown

Angel's trumpet essence is used for the times when life as we know it dramatically changes. It helps with all physical, emotional, and psychological transitions. This is a beneficial remedy for earthquake and tsunami survivors, as their entire world literally shifted and changed. Life as they know it is looks very different. Angel's trumpet is useful during any type of transition or death process. It helps us to look at the big picture and see the chain of events as our higher selves would see them.

This remedy is regarded as the "surrender" essence because it assists us in peaceful and profound transitions. It works to transmute the fear of death and destruction into the conscious awareness of our spiritual connections. It helps us to create the change from fear to transformation. Angel's trumpet essence is often used for letting go and crossing spiritual thresholds. It helps by opening our hearts to other realms and other experiences.

Angel's trumpet essence helps when we are trying to find the meaning in what is happening, when events around us literally boggle the mind — events that are so out of the ordinary that we don't even have the programming

for them. It helps us to find peace in surrendering to the unknown. Angel's trumpet essence is beneficial for working with hospice situations, emergencies, and other conditions of great stress and duress. It helps us figure out how to prioritize what the situation needs as opposed to what we think we need to give it. Using angel's trumpet essence helps our perception transcend into a new reality. It shows us how to joyfully surrender to whatever our next steps are. Angel's trumpet assists us in trusting the process of change. This is the birthing essence. We labor and deliver ourselves.

Aspen

Aspen essence is sometimes referred to as the "heebie-jeebies" essence. This essence is for the times when we know there are scary things out there, and we can't get a grasp on exactly what they are. It is as if all our anxieties are in a primordial fog of fear. We can feel them but we can't see them; they are just out of reach.

Quick Reference

- Calms anxiety
- Tames foreboding
- Aids high sensitivity
- Gives confidence in perception

This essence is perfect for when we feel fearful but do not know exactly where the fear is coming from. Aspen is indicated when it feels as if our fears are working against us rather than for us. It is the treatment for those times when our sensitivity and knowingness go rogue and we can't trust our judgment, when we have all the feelings of fear and trepidation but can't make sense of them, or when we just feel something ominous and looming.

Aspen essence acts as a balm for extrasensitivity. It assists us in processing and discerning all the seen and unseen information into something tangible and manageable. It gives us confidence in our perceptions. Aspen essence also provides an extra protective layer of energy. It enhances the perception and ability to connect with clarity and confidence. It supports the ability to filter out the feelings that don't serve us, allowing us to trust our feelings. It helps us by dialing down the fear so that we can discern what is real and what is reactive.

Aspen aids highly sensitive people to know what to trust and what not to trust. It teaches them to be mindful of their sensitive natures and shows them how to avoid getting flooded by all the input that overwhelms their ability to be discerning. Thus, aspen essence also helps with panic disorders. It provides a safety net by showing us how and what to pay attention to. Aspen essence works by helping us to have a high level of sensitivity and still be able to discriminate — and, more importantly, to feel safe in our own skins.

Aspen

California Poppy

Quick Reference

- Promotes inner development
- Focuses path to enlightenment
- Sorts substance from shine

California poppy essence is sometimes regarded as the "golden carrot" formula: "If I meditate for forty days and fast for forty nights, I will become enlightened, and all my goals will be achieved. I will be Godlike." But our enlightenment goals are ever elusive. This essence helps when we are attracted to all the spiritual fads and the latest gurus. It helps us to get a clue about what is real and how we can really get to where we want to go. It balances our energy so we are less attracted to those quick fixes to enlightenment. California poppy essence gets us in the right place — in the now and in the know.

This essence shows us the true light of our contributions. We can feel the value of what we have to offer. We feel our parts, no matter how big or how small. Our strength is in who we are and what our particular capacities are. It is enough to be ourselves. California poppy breaks the spell of charismatic influence. It validates who we are and what we do. Our work becomes more meaningful, as we have a deeper knowing of our place in the grand scheme of things.

Sometimes we become enmeshed in dream worlds outside of our own. California poppy balances that sense of being blinded by the light. As we seek our connections to God and Spirit, we can become lost in the drama of our own experiences. Whether we are praying, channeling, on a path with a guru, or beholden to some cause, California poppy sorts out the substance from the shine. It strengthens us by helping us to remember our own power. It helps us to do our own work, giving us a spiritual backbone.

We have to be willing to do the work to get the goodies. There is no secret for getting around what we are supposed to do for our purpose.

Canyon Dudleya

Quick Reference

- Promotes discernment
- Focuses on present
- Integrates insight and purpose
- Encourages practical spirituality

Canyon dudleya essence is tailor-made for the dramatic "I see Jesus" type of spiritual experience. Sometimes we can have the ultimate dramatic connection but then feel like asking, "Where do we go from there?" We are still on Earth, and as much as we may have gained huge insight into our souls and purpose, how do we make it meaningful? How do we integrate it into daily life? We can get so attached to the glamour of the experience that we lose focus about what the experience serves.

Canyon dudleya nourishes the soul by focusing on the here and now. It creates balance. This essence teaches us how to work with guidance and presence in a practical way. We eat, we sleep, we have fun, we work, we pray, and we are always connected. We do not have to continue to strive for the demonstrations of our psychic and spiritual connections, because we know that they already exist right here and right now. We are our experiences; we live them. They are who we are. We are the experience.

Columbine

Columbine essence is used for the times we lose ourselves in the plan. It helps us at the point in our lives when we have forgotten who we are. If we are highly identified with a job or a role, we sometimes lose our essence. We feel we have nothing more to give because we are all used up. We forget how to do, and we forget how to be. We just plain forget. Columbine wakes us back up. It allows us to tap back into who we are as individuals.

Quick Reference

- Helps us remember who we are
- Erases past burdens
- Inspires thought, action

Columbine is frequently called the "midlife crisis" essence. It is used particularly for that point in our lives when the stagnation or disappointment may take over and we don't know how to do a makeover. It rallies the creative forces and helps us to remember who we are and what we are capable of. I like to think of columbine as a magic eraser that helps to erase the burdens from the past.

This essence creates breakthroughs by helping us to take stock of the culmination of all our experiences to bless, appreciate, and learn. It creates movement through inspired thought and action. It helps us to remember how much we count, how much we know, and how much we contribute. Most of all, we get out of the mental and emotional prison of who we are and where we are supposed to be at any specific period in our lives. We remember. We connect. We reconnect. We work a new plan with a whole new premise.

Columbine

Deer Brush

Deer brush essence stimulates motivation by establishing clarity of purpose. We cannot achieve what we want if we have mixed intentions. Deer brush lends its focus to all that we do. It motivates through pure intention. It aligns us with our motives. If we are not congruent with what we want and how we go about getting it, then we will not achieve the desired result, and we'll get mixed results. With deer brush essence, we clearly see how the inner affects the outer. This essence motivates us to get clear and see what muddles the process.

Quick Reference

- Accesses authenticity
- Clears illusions
- Clarifies soul purity
- Enhances inner virtue
- Integrates thoughts, deeds

Fawn Lily

Fawn lily essence is for the fear of contaminating the delicate spirit. This is the "monk on the mountain" remedy. There are times when we can feel safe only when isolated or in our own spiritual or emotional routines, fearing outside influences that may sideline or distract us from our practice. Fawn lily helps to preserve our natural spiritual gifts among everyday people and everyday life. This essence reminds us that we have much to share. Spiritual gifts evolve through progress and vitality as well as communion with others. Fawn lily essence helps us to be more accepting and involved in world practices. We face fear through the sharing of knowledge.

Quick Reference

- Preserves natural spiritual gifts
- Promotes sharing knowledge
- Enhances vitality, connection
- Fosters acceptance, involvement

Fawn Lily

Gorse

Gorse essence is the "worth it" essence. It's used for the times when we don't want to participate in the future because it seems no effort is worth it and nothing will change. We can easily feel discouraged by situations from the past and feel that it is not worth investing in the future. So we hang out in the in-between space, not fully engaged in anything. Gorse essence helps by shining the light back in. It brings back the optimism in any future projections. This essence helps by making it worth it to invest our time.

Quick Reference

- Provides encouragement
- Brings optimism to future projections
- Reminds us it's worth it

Gorse

Gorse is used when we lose the fire in our bellies, for those times our pilot lights have gone out and no one and nothing provides the spark of motivation. We feel submerged in our hopelessness and despair. It is as if we are stuck in the basement of our emotions with a dim and dirty light. Nothing is clear and we have lost our way.

We use gorse essence when we have exhausted all our options and feel nothing else is working. It rallies our strength, hope, and resolve from a deep place in our souls. It shifts the concept of "what's the use?" to seeing, feeling, and embracing new prospects. Gorse essence is all about reaching up and seizing opportunity. It helps us align with our higher selves, guides, and angels and to not be limited by the version of what we think our options are. This essence reminds us to pay attention to the clues of a fresh new start.

Using this essence balances us by tipping the scales from despair to destiny. It automatically shifts our possibilities, allowing us to take stock of what obstacles and limitations we may have and then giving us the energy and wherewithal to move forward. We can stand tall in our abilities.

Lotus

Quick Reference

- Integrates spiritual and everyday lives
- Connects to higher consciousness
- Grounds visions

Lotus essence is a spiritual essence that helps us by expanding into our energy bodies and throughout our chakra systems. When we meditate too much or devote too much time to otherworldly concerns at the expense of our Earth lives, we can lose the very thing we wish to achieve and create: a deeper connection to our God and ourselves. Lotus blends well with other essences, such as angelica, to help with connecting to the divine. It is one of the components of my aura spray Divine Connection (see the Special Combinations chapter), which is used for prayer, dreams, and meditation purposes. It helps us to integrate all the aspects of our spiritual and daily lives. We cleanse and create by accessing the divine within.

Some of us overamplify our connection to the light that surrounds us and attempt to live in the higher realms at the expense of a balanced spirituality. We can sometimes take on a holier-than-thou attitude due

to our so-called enhanced spiritual consciousness. Lotus balances our spiritual forces. It helps to ground us and keeps us focused on harmonizing all of our energy centers. It works as a spiritual tonic to connect us to higher versions of consciousness. Lotus essence encourages the God particle to open and expand the insight of personal spirituality.

This essence is also useful for those of us who are so open and expanded that everyday life begins to feel unreal and irrelevant. Lotus essence has a way of balancing out the chakras so that we are more whole, connecting us to our guides and insights in a more profound manner. It helps us learn how to listen and how to become whole. Lotus clears and aligns the subtle bodies, adjusting and clearing the layers. We should think about using lotus essence as we would to upgrade programs on a computer. The old system might function for the programs it is designed to run, but when the programs become overloaded or limited in their scope, the system fails to perform properly. Lotus essence can upgrade our programming, putting in a "patch" for overall effectiveness.

Lotus helps us to integrate our crown chakras with our heart chakras. Lotus integrates the lofty aspects of the higher chakras with the heart. It makes heaven and its gifts more real and tangible. Spirituality becomes a living work in progress. We can feel both the love and Spirit, and now we experience them working together as one. Lotus helps us to reestablish our connection to Spirit. This is the "direct line to God" essence. We feel it. We become it. We are it.

Milkweed

> **Quick Reference**
> - Fosters healthy connections
> - Promotes awareness
> - Instills independence
> - Helps with substance dependency

Milkweed essence is for those times when we are feeling completely off track. It is sometimes known as the "escapist" essence. It works well for addictions and overdependence on anything in general. Milkweed is for anything we depend on aside from our guides or ourselves.

Sometimes we feel the need to make a connection at any cost. We need to feel *anything*. We need to connect to *something*. Whether it is food, drugs, sleep, or religion, we just need something. Milkweed essence helps us to connect by nourishing the soul with strength and self-reliance. We feel ourselves again because of who we are and how we relate in the world. We feel connected because we have a healthy sense of what we want. We learn to honor ourselves and our strengths. We are enough.

Mugwort

> **Quick Reference**
> - Integrates dreams
> - Expands perception
> - Balances consciousness
> - Integrates insights
> - Promotes links

Mugwort essence is a good balance for integrating our dreams and our daily lives. It allows for access to the vision as well as the execution of the vision. There are times when we are stuck in the properties of the dream — something that we can feel but is slightly out of reach. We can almost touch it and see it coming more into focus, and then the energy is not there to bring it into full expression. Mugwort grabs the dream and puts it into conscious action. Now our dreams can be as real as we want them to be.

Mugwort essence is known as a dream enhancer. It helps to balance the dream life with the waking life. It acts as a bridge between two or more states of being. This is an excellent essence to use during those times we have difficulty remembering our dreams. It helps us tune into dreamtime to access other aspects of our consciousnesses. Mugwort has multidimensional applications. On one level, it opens us to the value of psychic life and dreams. On another level, it guides and protects us from being overwhelmed by multidimensional information. This essence helps us to put all aspects of our insight into perspective. We receive knowledge and insight, and we also get the grounding of that knowledge and insight.

Note that mugwort is used in Chinese medicine for moxibustion. Moxibustion is a healing technique that helps to lock chi into acupuncture points to create more overall energy. It inspires bodily health.

Mugwort

Mullein

Quick Reference

- Builds relationship between conscience and body wisdom
- Infuses truth
- Awakens the inner voice

Mullein essence helps us to listen to our inner imperative. It incites cellular honesty. With it, we find that the more we listen to the cues from our inner cores, the more we feel supported by our world. Mullein essence is used for character building. It helps to create a personal relationship between our conscience and our body wisdom. Through its influence, we can appreciate what makes us who we truly are.

This essence is a personal inner-truth elixir. We become enough by knowing we are enough and that we no longer have to prove our worthiness. Mullein also helps to provide a strong moral compass. It has a way of tapping into the divine to give us a gauge for our personal fortitude and conviction. Mullein essence awakens the inner voice. With it, we can hear what is right and appropriate for us as we are aligned with Spirit. This is the essence of authenticity. It helps us to grow backbones and to take a stand for who we are and what is right for us. Mullein might sound a bit stodgy, but it provides a truer way of listening to that inner call. It makes situations relevant to us, allowing us to become our own leaders.

Mullein essence helps us to tune into our inner voices and consciences. This essence motivates us to be the best that we can be. How do we want

Mullein

Nasturtium

the world to be? How do we choose to participate? What can we do to make it better? In many ways, this is a listening remedy that won't let us get away with procrastinating about our roles or just sliding by. Mullein holds us accountable and will kick-start any resolutions we make.

Nasturtium

Quick Reference

- Escapes dogmatic thinking
- Helps creative thoughts
- Integrates vitality
- Promotes learning from experience

Do you get stuck in paralysis by analysis? Do you think through your feelings? Do you find that you are disconnected between your heart and your head? For the struggle between logic and emotion, nasturtium essence gets us out of the box. This is a great remedy for anyone who has to commit to dry, academic-like, or intricate material. It's for those of us who have a tendency to get stuck in one way of thinking or perceiving. We become so committed to working in the box that working out of the box fries our circuits and we lose our sense of intuitive mobility.

We get stuck on the simplest of questions, such as "How do you feel?" We think, "What do they mean by that? Is there something wrong with me?" Using nasturtium essence brings vitality back into our thinking and analytical processes. It reconnects our life forces so that all of our senses contribute to the decision-making process and we can trust enough to trust ourselves. We begin to feel our intellects and life experiences in a more balanced manner. We open to experience as its own education, separate from books or formulas. We start to live our lives more fully.

This essence is sometimes known as the thinker's formula. It works to get us out of our heads. We can sometimes think ourselves into a box, and by the time we think ourselves out of the box, we are no longer in touch with our feelings but rather how we are thinking about our feelings. "If it isn't in print, then it doesn't exist." Nasturtium essence teaches the necessity of the experiential. It is just as important to learn from experience as it is to learn from books. Experience gives balance to our knowledge and wisdom.

Nasturtium essence is an important remedy to get us into our bodies and see that they are not just there as support for our heads. We can use this remedy for those times when it feels as if we have been studying for hours and we're still stuck on one particular problem. It will help change the way we are thinking and can create a much-needed creative breakthrough.

Quaking Grass

Quick Reference

- Helps recognize self
- Adjusts energy in group situations
- Brings natural harmony

Flower essences have the innate capacity to restore us to our highest vibration and sense of connection. Quaking grass works well when we feel dysfunctional in a group setting. This essence adjusts our energy, both when we are so strong that we feel we can receive nothing from others and also when we are so withdrawn that we feel we have nothing to contribute.

I like to use quaking grass around the holidays, as it helps us to recognize ourselves and connect with others within group settings, such as with family, business associates, and friends. This essence brings about natural harmony and reminds us of who we are in relation to others. Quaking grass essence helps us to remember the big picture and what part we need to play.

Queen Anne's Lace

Queen Anne's Lace

Quick Reference

- Connects to higher insight
- Balances observation
- Enhances clarity, clairvoyance

Queen Anne's lace essence helps us learn how to open to higher levels of consciousness. We benefit from this essence by obtaining access to clear insights to help us remove emotional and intellectual debris. It is traditionally used to steady spiritual openings and enhance natural clairvoyance. Queen Anne's lace remedy restructures the ability to tap into our innate psychic abilities. It creates resonance between the spiritual and earthly energies, helping us ground our connections with the divine into the everyday. It gives a platform for connecting to higher insight and abilities. Queen Anne's lace provides benefit to the God particle by enhancing confidence and clarity with intuitive insights as it helps us to "see."

This essence helps with distortions in our vision. It enhances our clairvoyance by clearing out the astral and emotional debris, which can cloud our insight. It is particularly useful for intuitives and other lightworkers. It provides true clarity. Queen Anne's lace essence has a grounding effect on intuition. Guidance comes from how we integrate our information, and this essence aligns the guidance process by cleansing and purifying any imbalances in the system. The result is trueness to what we see. We *know* it is true for us; we can *feel* the truth of it.

Rock Water

> **Quick Reference**
> - Navigates spiritual discipline
> - Restores flexibility in pursuits
> - Goes with the flow

Rock water essence helps us when we believe that following some strict regimen will bring us closer to God. Some spiritual practices dictate that the more we pray, fast, meditate, or _____, the stronger the guarantee of enlightenment. It is our nature to want to do more, be more, and have more, and the belief here is that this will give us an express ticket to heaven. Rock water essence aids us in navigating the fine line between having a spiritual discipline and being a dogmatic martyr for the cause. This is the essence to use for the times we deny our human need to achieve a closer relationship to God.

There are times when we are very disciplined in our habits, but the sense of serenity and accomplishment we long for still eludes us. In response, we seek to do even more of "all the right things." Yet the more we continue to do "right," the more "wrong" it continues to feel, and we become exhausted. Rock water essence restores a sense of flexibility. Rather than investing in how we think we "should" be and how we think we "should" experience, we begin to trust our own guidance. Rock water essence erodes the hard edges of rigidity. It smoothes the surfaces, transforming through gentleness. This essence puts the "person" into the personal. The experience of our lives is valuable. We no longer feel the need to conform to how we should be — as a doctor, lawyer, Indian chief, or whatever the case might be.

Rock water remedy also helps those of us who are following a strict dietary discipline — whether vegan, core balance, Atkins, or macrobiotic. This essence reminds us that extreme denial isn't the passkey to heaven. Spiritual enlightenment recognizes the time and place for all extensions of God. That chocolate bar, velvet comforter, or sensual touch is a reminder of the sweetness of life just as much as prayer, angelic guidance, and deprivation. Rock water essence is about balancing all aspects of life and consciousness. It teaches us to be in the flow of life rather than damming the river. It shows us how the rock is warmed in the sun to provide warmth, comfort, and structure for Spirit. The water flows when and where it needs to go.

Scotch-Broom

Scotch-broom essence is for those whose worldview is one of impending doom and the sense that the world is ending. When reality feels as if it consists of nothing but impending doom — and we can feel the sheer weight of all of the negativity portrayed all over the world — we tend to feel that nothing we do will ever make a difference. Many times, we feel powerless in the face of world events and can easily tap into sadness and despair. We might feel addicted to CNN or any of the 24–7 news channels, following to the nth detail any war or major upset that continues to feed our growing unease and despair.

Quick Reference

- Restores optimism
- Brings a sense of purpose
- Promotes perspective
- Fights collective despair

Scotch-Broom

Using scotch-broom essence restores a sense of optimism and service. It helps us remember that we are all connected and that every little thought, gesture, or intention can make a difference. Scotch-broom revives the power of one. This essence can bring a sense of purpose, allowing us to feel the effects of our contributions.

Shasta Daisy

> **Quick Reference**
> - Restores wholeness
> - Emulsifies life
> - Reintegrates experiences
> - Elevates point of view
> - Aids in problem solving

Shasta daisy essence is the integration essence. It creates a new foundation to include the integration of all modalities and to promote substance and positive evolution. It addresses a freedom from fear or, more importantly and perhaps more realistically, a freedom to feel the fear and do things anyway. Shasta daisy essence teaches us to balance feelings with intellect, following the credo that each serves a valuable function. One is not better than the other.

This essence is a great formula for "getting it." It is an "aha!" catalyst. We often get so caught up in the individual parts, questioning how they are supposed to connect, we can easily lose the connection of the whole. Shasta daisy can take us out of ourselves so we can see things in entirely new configurations. It helps us by enhancing our viewpoint to include all the contributing factors. This essence elevates our point of view as if we are looking at our issues through a telescope. Depending on where you are, the entire landscape changes. This essence allows you to repattern and reinterpret your emotional landscape.

Shasta daisy is also a useful remedy for bringing seemingly disparate healing modalities together. Inspiration comes from its ability to see from a higher perspective of connection. I like to think of this formula as providing the view of how Spirit sees the interplay of our projects and inspirations. This remedy aids any process for creativity and problem solving.

Shooting Star

Quick Reference

- Promotes belonging
- Addresses feeling different
- Utilizes planetary energies
- Connects to Earth

Shooting star essence is for those of us who have never felt a part of anything, for those who feel a profound sense of alienation or a disconnect from feeling human. When all the little things that make people feel like part of something do not seem to make any sense to us at all — they are either meaningless or seem to take too much effort — the shooting star remedy can aid us in finding our way back, allowing each of us to be a participant and enjoy the simple pleasures that are available. There is a great comfort in knowing who we are.

Many of us feel disconnected or not at home; perhaps we have never felt a connection to Earth. We might feel a strong pull toward extraterrestrial stories or visions of life in other worlds. Human life might seem

alien and chaotic. When we feel this way, shooting star essence addresses that deep longing for home and belonging. Shooting star releases the feeling of being trapped in this life on Earth. This remedy teaches us how to utilize the planetary energies in an Earth-based system and how to connect through the heart and the body as a container for Spirit.

Star-Tulip

Quick Reference

- Attunes to Spirit and insight
- Helps determine purpose
- Softens overprotective armor
- Helps with listening

Star-tulip essence opens up our ears and eyes to the God within. It helps us attune to the subtleties of Spirit and insight. It enhances all capacities for meditation, prayers, and intuition. Star-tulip essence dissolves the harsh coating that some of us use to protect ourselves. This type of protection effectively cuts us off from the ability to intuit and discern insight. Star-tulip essence makes it safe for us to listen to what we need to hear. This remedy acts as an emotional and spiritual emulsifier. It works by blending all the elements necessary for healing and intuition, clearing the way for personal contact and connection to Source.

This essence is often referred to as a "tuning in" remedy. It helps us to

determine what our particular purpose is. It prepares us. It enhances all of our intuitive abilities: prayer, meditation, dreams, and visioning. Star-tulip is most helpful when we are in that gray area and nothing seems to be coming forth. We draw a blank, and the inspiration comes from the blankness itself. There are no preconceived notions. Star-tulip forces us to trust our imaginations. It eliminates the distractions by not allowing us access to what will cloud our vision. We will have the inner knowing of what real inspiration is and what mind chatter is.

Star-tulip is also known as "cat's ears." It helps us breach the barriers to expanded awareness and consciousness. It reminds us that guidance and the higher versions of ourselves are always available. The delicate qualities of cat's ears remind us to listen with our own "cat ears," tuning into all inner insight and the intricacies of movement within.

When we are fearful of what we should be doing and how we should be doing it, fearing the world is unsafe, we go into psychic lockdown mode and can no longer "hear." All we hear is fear. Star-tulip helps us to open up and perceive. We are no longer limited by our reactions to ominous outside threats but instead feel innate guidance and personal directives. Fear is faced through inner attunement and guidance. If we feel that it is difficult to pray or meditate and are easily distracted by all that is going on, star-tulip helps us to receive insights. Star-tulip essence works by softening the protective layer that prevents us from being able to receive.

Sweetpea

Quick Reference

- Creates a sense of belonging
- Fosters community connection
- Helps with moving

Sweetpea is known as the "stranger in a strange land" remedy. It works well when we are moving into a new area and don't have a personal history to share with others. It has the ability to lock in that sense of belonging and feeling of home. This essence brings with it a sense of commitment to something greater than ourselves. It grounds and stabilizes when we have to move or are feeling disconnected from our current home. It works by creating "home" where we are, lending peace and a sense of belonging. Use this essence when you move to a new place or feel homesick. It connects us to our current geography.

Water Violet

Water violet essence is used for the reserved among us, those who hold back who they are. Some of us might feel a distance between ourselves and others. The indication for water violet essence is appearing aloof and reserved. We might be perceived as stuck-up and above it all. This is a gross misrepresentation. We just don't know how to participate. The simplest exchanges can feel awkward and unnatural. Water violet helps ease our paths as we learn how to share with others.

Quick Reference

- Breaks down walls of detachment
- Accentuates independence and interdependence
- Instills humanity

Each of us has a unique contribution to share. Water violet essence breaks down the wall of detachment, allowing active participation while still keeping adequate personal boundaries. This essence is extremely helpful for intuitives, therapists, and channels. It prevents the tendency to withdraw further into the self. Water violet helps us to feel more connected. It helps the ice around our hearts to thaw, allowing our natural gentleness to come through. We allow people to see and feel who we are. We allow ourselves to flow with others. Water violet essence accentuates our independence and interdependence. We feel the value of us being ourselves.

Yellow Star-Tulip

Yellow star-tulip essence has a similar quality to star-tulip essence and assists our learning to receive as well as adding a more empathetic component to life. Yellow star-tulip is excellent for teachers and practitioners of the healing arts, as it adds a deep and comprehensive understanding directly from Source. It allows us to see from broader views, gaining higher access to intuition and information.

Quick Reference

- Develops empathy
- Restores compassion
- Refines sensitivity
- Helps step outside of self

Yellow star-tulip is often regarded as a learning essence. It makes us pay attention and take notes, remembering that there is much to be gained by learning how to listen and that there are many ways to listen and receive. Yellow star-tulip also works well with self-absorption, which can often prevent us from really having a clue about others. It takes us out of ourselves so that we can see truly without constantly looking through the filter of how things are going to affect us.

CHAPTER FOUR

Manifestation

There is always a divine hand in inspiration, as we are creations of Spirit and divinely guided. Inspiration, motivation, and creativity are all intricately connected. Inspiration is that spark that drives us to be, to know, and to create. We can always feel when it is at work.

Blackberry

Quick Reference

- Instills motivation
- Helps initiate change
- Gives necessary "oomph"
- Enhances other essences

Blackberry is often regarded as the "get off your butt and get to it!" essence. It catalyzes anything we do. It translates energy into form. We all have ideas, desires, dreams, and wishes. Blackberry essence removes obstacles of thought and organizes energy to manifest the will to action and deeds. This formula gets us out of the purely mental realm and into the realm of action and execution.

Blackberry is the remedy to use to help us initiate necessary changes. It is the motivator essence. Think about the very nature of a blackberry bush: Its branches are filled with thorns and delicious berries. They are tangled together, making it difficult to reach in and pluck the berries without intense determination, focus, and some scratches to show for our efforts. We can get so distracted by the entanglements that even when we see the bright, shiny berries, we don't know how to get started.

We might be fearful of doing the necessary work. Blackberry essence reminds us that we have to start somewhere. It shows us that we can get those berries if we cut through the branches and pluck what we want, and it keeps us from stalling out. One of the challenges with the manifestation process is that we can see what we want but we don't have enough juice to actualize it; we somehow get trapped in our heads. Blackberry essence creates success by helping us translate our dreams into realities.

I love to work with blackberry, as it has the ability to boost other essences as well, so whether we are working with confidence, focus, enthusiasm, or decisiveness, blackberry adds rocket fuel to what we want. This essence puts us back in the driver's seat. We see whatever obstacles or challenges are ahead, and we look for the solutions rather than focusing on the problems. Blackberry powers whatever we want to put into action. All we have to do is follow through on the thought process. Blackberry essentially gives us the "oomph" necessary to do whatever it is we want to do. It gets us out of our heads and onto our feet.

Calendula

Quick Reference

- Softens communication
- Creates space for listening
- Aids in relationship work

Calendula essence is used for the times we use cutting words and demonstrate argumentative behavior. People tend to respond to tone rather than words, and assumptions are made about one's character because of the tone of one's voice. Calendula essence works by softening that tone. This is a great essence for communication because it helps to release a lot of the pent-up aggression that comes from reacting to tone. Calendula essence increases warmth and active communication. It opens us to using our voices as tools to connect and soothe so that our words create connection rather than argumentative distancing; they caress and create new avenues for exchange.

Calendula

Whereas snapdragon helps with words that just seem to fly out of the mouth, calendula is used for words that are deliberately cutting to make a point or to have some kind of control. Oftentimes, we don't mean to say what we say or to deliver our words in such a negative way; it just seems to come out that way. Conversation often degrades into argument at these times, but we can't seem to help it because we feel the need to make that point.

Calendula essence opens up the channel of communication through words. It lends its own receptivity. This remedy also works well when we are in direct contact with someone who has a dragon tongue. It helps to create the space for active listening and a more generous response. When using this essence, we feel the lines of communication blossom in an elegant and effortless manner. We become willing to receive the "word" for our peace and for the peace and comfort of others. This is also an excellent remedy for relationship work because its major gift is the gift of receiving others.

Cayenne

Cayenne flower essence breaks up stagnation, and it is an important remedy when we are feeling stuck in life. Whether we are procrastinating or cannot get the energy up to get motivation, cayenne creates a new pathway. It works well for when we know we are complacent and don't know what to do about it. It energizes anything we do.

Quick Reference

- Breaks up stagnation
- Catalyzes work
- Supercharges changes
- Promotes progress
- Creates new pathways

Cayenne essence is sometimes regarded as the "wake up and smell the coffee" formula. It shakes us out of the comfy cocoon of complacency. It reminds us that we are here to grow and to be all we can be. It breaks us out of any pattern of inertia. It encourages us to seek new experiences for our growth and delight. Cayenne essence is a catalyst. It works well with any other essence to supercharge changes. It literally adds spice and movement to our lives, transforming us by breaking up internal patterns of crystallization so we can move freely again. Cayenne essence wakes us to the window of change and transformation.

Not only is cayenne a powerful catalyst that nullifies complacency,

Cayenne

but it can also be used specifically to catapult us from one phase to the next. Cayenne kicks us out of our comfort zones, ready or not. It works very well when we are nervous or hesitant about taking that next step. It helps us in those times when we know what we should do but we have trepidation about what the change will look like.

This essence opens our eyes to what is possible. It is a remedy for all life changes. Cayenne essence helps us remember our particular spice — not just the nice — and it creates success by helping us embrace change. It has a way of creating new pathways to the future. It activates anything we are working on and gives us movement and positive direction.

Clematis

Quick Reference

- Wakes daydreamers
- Helps make dreams reality
- Enriches creativity
- Awakens senses
- Focuses on now

Clematis essence is indicated when we are living through the dream of our future selves. There are times when we can see ourselves with a certain position or a certain mate or even a certain lifestyle, yet we cannot see a way to get there. This goes on inside our heads, and we don't take any steps to live our futures. Clematis helps us to put our dreams into our feet and our feet into reality. Through using this essence, all of the visions and dreams that flow so easily through our heads now get redirected and centered into walking our paths. This essence makes us pay attention to where we are, where we are going, and most importantly, how we are going to get there. It puts the dream into reality by opening the window to the now.

This essence works by fortifying and strengthening the creative cords of vision and inspiration into a workable plan or pieces. It helps us see the value of imagination and how to effectively use our creative clarity, so it's great for artists and writers needing to put forth the projects trapped in their heads onto paper or canvas. It awakens our senses and makes us much more aware of who we are and how we are. It can make our dreaminess work for us by helping us to see things in a new way.

During those times when we're in some kind of coma — emotional, food-related, or otherwise — clematis nudges us back into the present, allowing us to be ready, willing, and able to take action. It is a "just do it" formula, which makes it great for procrastinators. Clematis can light the necessary fire under our butts. This essence also makes our timing work for us. Using clematis makes us feel that as soon as we put a thought into action, a safety net will appear. However, it is the initial action that creates the process of being supported. When we use clematis, we find ourselves taking more interest in the here and now as it becomes more intriguing than our dream worlds. We begin to see the benefits of participating in our lives.

Clematis

I have used this remedy successfully with sinus and allergy problems. Allergies, as well as other illnesses, can make us feel trapped or limited, alone in our own physical worlds. I have found that clematis helps to break the energy of feeling limited by our symptoms.

Cosmos

Quick Reference

- Brings substance to creative force
- Helps articulate
- Makes sense of things
- Clarifies expression

Cosmos essence is one of my personal favorites. This is a great remedy for writers or people who work with words or in other areas of creativity. The best way I can describe this essence is to say that it helps you pull out a word or concept and develop it into a cohesive piece of work. For example, we have all these pieces and each sounds good on its own, but now we have to pull them all together. The words get lost because we don't know how to connect the dots, and we get frustrated because our words seem to lose their magic.

Cosmos essence organizes and makes sense of it all. Maybe things do not come together exactly as we thought they would, but now they make more sense. This essence takes our creative force and grounds it into

substance. It helps us to execute our projects. Cosmos helps us to look at our words and say, "That sounds better than I thought!"

This essence is essential for interpreting all the downloads that are coming through. Many of us are receiving vast quantities of information through connections with prayer, insight, and meditation. Cosmos essence allows us to articulate what we see and feel. It helps us to make sense of our senses. It changes our focus from feeling overwhelmed and swirling in chaos to getting the big picture. Cosmos essence maneuvers us through deciphering and managing all our information. We soon find that we have the right words, the right timing, and the right clarity. Cosmos helps us in those times when what we are expressing does not seem to be a true representation of what we really think or feel, when all we feel is the stumble of the thought jumble.

It helps us to sort, refine, and access what we need to know and what we need to share with others. We begin to feel the connections coming through in a guided way. We love the way it feels to know and to speak our truth. With cosmos's help, our words flow and make sense. We may even find that as we speak and think, there is great clarity in the quality of our expression. Cosmos essence lets our voices and words shine through with soul authenticity. Using cosmos is a great way to "defrag" our brains. I like this essence because it creates flow and helps keep us in sync.

Fairy Lantern

Quick Reference

- Fertilizes personal growth
- Helps us grow up
- Fosters maturity
- Helps us value growth

Fairy lantern essence is commonly used for the mother who wants her children to remain needy and dependent. This type of mother doesn't want her children to grow up. There are times when we may feel that we can only get love and acceptance by remaining the same, and so we create an artificially static state of being to obtain the love we need. Fairy lantern essence addresses this stunted process of development. It acts as fertilizer for our personal growth, teaching us how to be safe on our own and allowing us to bloom and flourish.

Fairy lantern essence is also used for that feeling of "not quite there

yet." It can help us when we feel immature or childlike and not quite up to the task of living a full and empowered life. We might find ourselves playing the waiting game. This game traps us in repetitions of "never now but maybe later," because we feel that we are never quite up to the task as we lack the value of our own direction. Fairy lantern essence addresses the helplessness and neediness that comes out of not trusting our abilities. It encourages the value of our contributions and our unique worth. This essence helps us to grow up and take stock of who we are and to value our own growth processes.

Impatiens

Impatiens is tailor-made for our contemporary society. Do you find yourself cutting people off in traffic and in midsentence? Do lines make you crazy? Impatiens is the essence that helps us slow down and listen. It allows us to pace ourselves. We can rush to be first and be fastest, but then

Quick Reference

- Slows things down
- Helps align with flow, purpose
- Lends a sense of priority

what? Where are we? This essence helps to release the internal tension that can cause burnout. It has a way of making us even more effective because we are not so attached to where we need to go but can instead focus on how to get there — and how to "be there" when we get there. Impatiens essence lends us a sense of priority, allowing us to put things into perspective.

It helps at times when we finish other people's sentences, when we can't wait for the punch line or the end of a story, or when we might even get irritated with the manner in which someone is speaking. We feel like we want to literally pull their words out. We are returning the answer before they've asked the question. Conversely, impatiens also helps when we are impatient speakers. We are able to focus more clearly and respond appropriately feeling the essence of true communication. Impatiens essence helps us to pause — to stop and take a breath. It settles the nerves.

This essence doesn't necessarily make us more patient, but it does change our perception of how things should flow and go. It helps us respect how others pace themselves. Impatiens stops that feeling of exhaustion that comes from not being in the right place at the right time. This essence helps us to align with flow and purpose and stop being angry and irritated all the time. It primes us to deal with our sense of urgency in a crisis and slows down the mad scramble of the thought process. Impatiens relaxes the internal tension that comes from the urgings of "how, where, and why do I need to react next?" This essence works by dialing down the urgent response and relaxing some of the tension. It also helps us tolerate the rhythms of others so that we can work with them rather than against them.

Impatiens is also a good essence to use for the times we feel that we are not healing fast enough and that all our therapies are not getting us anywhere. Part of the healing process is to slow down so that we can pay attention. The impatiens essence can help to reset our pace. It can give us the patience we need to be aware of what our bodies and souls are trying to tell us. It provides an opening so that we can see what is working for us and what isn't.

I like to use impatiens essence for creativity issues. It addresses the restlessness of trying to get things right and get them done fast enough. The brain and the body can't keep up with each other. The restlessness drives the creativity, but the creativity suffers from the restlessness. It doesn't have a proper direction. It is there, and we can feel it knocking on the door, but it doesn't have a home yet. Impatiens essence can give the creative drive a home. It helps by slowing things down a bit, so we can breathe and see what is needed and where.

Impatiens essence is also great for the holidays. We can use it when there is too much to do and we have to deal with others' schedules. There are days when we don't feel well during the holiday season, and our cold or flu seems to just drag on and on. We can feel amped and irritated by the rhythms of others. Impatiens essence helps us to breathe and to participate in the present time. With this essence, we can enjoy the moments and learn from the rhythms of others. Children benefit greatly from it, especially when they are counting the days before they can open their presents!

Indian Paintbrush

Quick Reference

- Gives form to intentions
- Enhances creativity
- Brings in vitality
- Raises consciousness

Indian paintbrush essence sparks possibility into productivity. This remedy reminds us that seeing life as a work of art compels us to do something; our very nature is to create. We stumble and limit ourselves by defining creativity for artists and painters. Indian paintbrush essence teaches us that our lives are our creations, and we have many tools at our disposal.

This essence establishes a current for us to utilize all of our resources. It generates exuberance in our problem solving. Creativity by its very nature is an essence. Take the raw materials of ability, emotion, and need or desire. Add some exuberance and gusto, think of something impossible, and you have your next step. This essence springs us forward by tapping into our personal current of creative productivity.

Indian paintbrush essence enhances creativity. It is also the essence for any kind of creative block. We can use it when we are stuck — when we can't think of the first word, can't pick the perfect color, or can't think outside the box. It is liquid inspiration. This remedy also gets us out of a rut — when we feel "blah" and see no forward movement in sight. Indian paintbrush brings in vitality and has a way of turning inspiration into reality. It gives form to our intentions.

This essence has an energy factor to aid in the creative process of making things more tangible. With the aid of this essence, we know we can do it. We feel it. We see it. We make it. We literally breathe life into our creations. This essence makes projects real for us. It is great for manifestation. It brings together heaven and Earth.

Iris

Iris essence is the essence of pure inspiration. This remedy inspires by constructing a bridge between spirit and matter. At times, we become stuck in our routines; each day seems too similar to the day before it, and soon there is nothing much to look forward to. Some of us live in the realm of dreams, focusing all of our attention on how things should be without making any effort to create our dreams.

Quick Reference

- Enables full self-expression
- Enhances vitality
- Gives new perception
- Revitalizes senses

Iris essence restores our ability to fully express ourselves. It helps us by utilizing the divine inspirations of our dreams to create a conduit to materialize them into something tangible. One of the attributes that strikes me about this essence is how it liberates us from the weight of the mundane or what is characterized as "normal." This alliance that we may think we need to make in order to succeed can end up stalling our forward movement. Iris essence springs us forward by enhancing our natural exuberance and vitality.

When we are bogged down by the mundane and feel that nothing good can come of our current circumstances, iris essence looks to heaven. It is similar to the lotus in the sense that it helps us to see something

Iris

beautiful rising from the muck and mire. It naturally elevates our vision and reconnects us with our divine selves. Iris works well in conjunction with Indian paintbrush (as sort of a dynamic duo) to break through any type of creative block. Iris connects us with the source, whereas Indian paintbrush gives us the physical vehicle for expression.

Iris essence inspires by showing us how to see in another light or perspective. So much is created by looking at circumstances from another viewpoint. Painters know the trick of turning their paintings upside down or reflecting them in a mirror to see the painting in a completely new way. Iris essence can give us this new view. We see what is going on or what we are dealing with at the time, and we no longer feel limited by whatever the existing problem or challenge is. We can see the light, and the light sees us. Iris essence gives us wings. Freedom comes from flying above our fears and challenges.

Joshua Tree

Joshua is the remedy that helps us to break ancestral patterns. We change ourselves by changing the energy of momentum and expectation. When we change our reactions and our expectations, we change the directions of our lives. Joshua tree essence breaks through the past to create the future for the new and the now.

Quick Reference

- Breaks ancestral patterns
- Clears karma
- Builds lineage
- Transforms family

Larkspur

Quick Reference

- Inspires leadership
- Helps us motivate and encourage others
- Clarifies reasons to lead

The essence of larkspur, also known as delphinium, is the leadership essence. As we strive and find our influence, we can become distorted by our intention. We might reach a certain pinnacle and feel that we have nothing left to learn or that no one can teach us anything. We could become limited by our own vision and get stuck in feelings of self-importance or of being overburdened by our duties and obligations to others. Larkspur helps us to find our way by allowing us to be inspired from within.

With larkspur, we can feel the shift in our personal consciousness from needing to be the boss to radiating the light of the way so that others will naturally want to follow. This essence creates a very empowering quality of acceptance — the acceptance of our gifts and talents as well as the acceptance of how to share those gifts and talents. It makes us step up, take notice, and look at the bigger picture. Larkspur essence serves us well when we are making personal quantum leaps. It helps us to acknowledge our responsibilities to others by being the best we can be and sharing our light.

Larkspur essence also helps us work through the filter of leadership. How are you supposed to lead? Do you lead for personal purposes? Do you feel burdened by responsibilities? Do you feel your vision is the only

vision? Larkspur essence helps us to find our place of true service. We feel the power of our inner ideals. Larkspur shows us how to lead for the right reasons. It helps us to align with the energy and enthusiasm to motivate and encourage others. We become the example of how we want to lead.

Lupine

Quick Reference

- Balances individual needs
- Integrates singular goals with groups
- Brings focus to group needs

Lupine essence is for the times when we are consumed with our own version of the plan. We work on the plan at our expense and at the expense of others. We are committed and devoted to the letter of the plan rather than the intent of the plan. Lupine essence works by broadening our horizons. It helps us to experience how our participation affects the whole. We are no longer an island working independently of others; we see how our butterfly wings create climate changes in unforeseen areas.

Lupine essence may also be helpful for the "monks on the mountain" among us. We can see clearly and experience the greater truths, but how do we translate those truths into day-to-day life with people, places, and things? Lupine can help translate those more lofty and singular goals to benefit all of us so that we can evolve our plans in a profound manner.

Madia

Madia essence is the typical formula used for lack of focus. This remedy is great to use when our thoughts and energies are scattered. It is indicated for those times that are not so much about a lack of focus but the application of our focus here, there, and everywhere. Madia essence acts like the lens of a camera, pulling all the elements into a comprehensive picture.

Quick Reference

- Enhances focus
- Directs attention
- Helps zero in on desires
- Increases concentration

When our thoughts are flustered and jumbled, we cannot create or articulate what our intentions are. This essence counteracts that scattered feeling by showing us how to prioritize and perceive in a more focused manner. We become more centered, allowing our awareness to work for us rather than against us. Madia essence helps us to aim the spotlight on what we want and how to get it. It helps us to use our time and space wisely. This is a great essence for that 2:00 to 3:00PM slump when we struggle with our next step.

Madia is an excellent "butterfly" essence — for when we flit from one subject to another. It helps us to zero in on what we want, whether that is simply concentration or something particular we want to manifest. When we use this essence, we feel the value of knowing and the value of paying attention. It lends its energy of pure focus to accomplish mental and physical goals. We can use our words to be precise and clear about what we desire to create. Our words then become cocreators.

Mallow

Quick Reference

- Breaks barriers
- Inspires reaching out
- Brings warmth of connection
- Encourages sharing

Mallow essence helps us to move beyond barriers. We might feel socially insecure and not trust what life is offering. This essence works well for those times when we limit our contact with others because we don't feel up to the task of reaching out. Mallow essence inspires us to reach out and become part of something greater. This is the social remedy that gives us the strength and confidence to fully participate as ourselves. We love the feeling of sharing our brilliance with open and warm hearts. Mallow essence helps us to receive and to reach out to others. As a result, we feel our value skyrocket through the beauty of sharing.

This formula is used for the socially awkward. Whether the barriers are social or cultural, this essence teaches how to reach out to others. It is the barrier breaker. It breaks down walls around the heart so there is once again a natural, effortless exchange of energy. This essence brings a feeling of the warmth of connection but also eliminates the fear of having to hold back parts of yourself.

Mountain Pride

Mountain Pride

> **Quick Reference**
> - Helps take charge
> - Fosters positive change
> - Inspires self-confidence
> - Turns inactions in to actions

Mountain pride essence helps us to take charge — to kick butt and take names. This is known as the "take a stand" formula. It assists us in rising to all challenges. We feel the strength of believing in our convictions when we use this essence. Mountain pride transforms our inactions into actions. Our convictions and beliefs are no longer some generic concept of what we may believe but a dynamic living energy to be shared. We feel ourselves fortified by the right use of will and willingness to fully participate. Mountain pride essence helps us to transform into positive forces for change.

This essence encourages us to believe in who we are and to be inspired by our ideals. When using it, we have the strength to be ourselves. We see adversity for what it is: a challenge. We are no longer limited by doubt and disillusion. I like one of the descriptions of the remedy in the *Flower Essence Repertory*: "It is an important remedy for those who confuse peace with passivity." Mountain pride is the essence for the spiritual warrior. It is used in many yang formulas, adding juju to all that we do. We become motivated as possibilities are made real through real action.

Penstemon

> **Quick Reference**
> - Supports victor mentality
> - Relieves harshness
> - Injects courage
> - Makes individuality feel safe

Penstemon essence is used for those times when we feel that we are working against the odds. This essence is indicated when no matter what we do, all our efforts and ideas are met with resistance. This isn't the garden-variety "let's challenge our commitment" essence; rather, it is the essence for the times when we feel that anything we do is met with adversity. Penstemon essence reminds us of our great inner fortitude. It helps us recognize the value of our experiences. It assists us to persevere and hold out for what we hold dear and true.

Penstemon supports us through the most trying of times, especially when the circumstances feel unfair or unjust. It helps us fight the good fight in spite of the challenges. The indications for taking penstemon essence are unfairness and undue burden. Penstemon essence reminds us that personal adversity is a tempering process. This remedy helps us to transform from the mentality of a victim to that of a victor by surviving

Penstemon

and learning from our circumstances. It gives us the strength to endure and helps to cultivate peace and productivity with the ability to prevail.

This is a good essence to use during those times we are feeling sorry for ourselves. Penstemon essence helps us so that we no longer feel that we need to personalize our pain. We feel safe being ourselves within our relationships. We don't have to so fiercely protect who we are and what we are doing, and we are no longer defined by pain.

Peppermint

Quick Reference

- Revitalizes mental process
- Stimulates brain
- Awakens perception
- Helps digestion
- Balances energy

Peppermint essence is for sluggish, uninspired thinking. It is for the couch potato who doesn't want to think of anything else except, "Should I have popcorn or pizza?" It is for the dullness that comes from not having to use the brain at all. This essence is traditionally used to "pep up" our thinking. It is indicated when we need that after-dinner boost, and it helps to revitalize and refresh the entire mental process.

If we feel that we have brain drain or as if not all our lights are working, peppermint essence can turn the juices back on, allowing us to feel a new approach or freshness in our thinking. Peppermint

Peppermint

essence works when our thought processes have been reduced to multiple choices. Think about how clearly we think after large holiday meals: All of our intellectual processes are rendered dormant to aid in our overall digestion. Peppermint essence inspires us to manage, digest, and access our intellectual thought processes. It breaks down food for thought so that it can all assimilate. It gets us off the couch and back into life.

Peppermint essence balances energy. It helps to integrate our thinking and our digestive processes by helping us to digest our thoughts so that they become clearer and more accessible. We feel more present in our bodies and more alert when we are thinking and studying.

Poison Oak

Quick Reference

- Mediates boundaries
- Gives strength to be vulnerable
- Clarifies personal space

Poison oak essence is used to mediate overly aggressive and angry boundaries. There are times when we may ferociously guard our space, even daring people to cross the line. We may not want to touch anyone or have anyone touch us. We tell ourselves that we are fine just being alone and in our own space — thank you very much. We feel that it's a hassle to have to put up with others. Such anger is about protecting ourselves and protecting our space.

Using poison oak essence diminishes the need for hostile boundaries.

We already feel intact, so this essence gives us the strength to be vulnerable. We know we can be supported by the very nature of who we are, so we no longer need all that barbed wire around our emotional bodies. Our protective field comes from our ability to discern what is true and good for us, allowing us to feel strong enough to be soft.

Pomegranate

Pomegranate essence is most often used for birthing, so I like to use it for giving birth to projects and aspects of self. It helps to bring forth hidden talents and gives them a home. It helps us to see that all is integrated rather than separate and that creativity lies in that integration rather than the separation. Nurturing and creativity are not mutually exclusive. Pomegranate essence gets us in touch with our own life cycles, allowing us to use them to create in the most powerful and effective ways. We become more fluid about what role we want to serve at any given time. Pomegranate also helps with emotional flexibility.

Quick Reference

- Balances femininity
- Manages creative impulses
- Helps with emotional flexibility
- Restores juiciness

Pomegranate

Rabbitbrush

Rabbitbrush essence is great for the student with too many projects and not enough time. It helps with those feelings of being overwhelmed or not knowing where to start and when to finish. This essence allows us to sort out the details of what is important and what needs to wait. Rabbitbrush assists us by showing us the bigger picture, letting us see that some projects are more detail oriented while others may need to retain an overview. We feel our confidence soar, and we recognize what is appropriate for every project.

Quick Reference

- Eases overwhelm
- Helps sort details
- Shows the bigger picture
- Keeps the mind flexible

Red Larkspur

Red larkspur is the essence for inspired leadership, and leadership that comes from knowing value begins from within. This essence infuses us with the vital forces of action and activity. It operates from the filter of "being all we can be" with energetic backup. We feel the life force and direction infuse into all that we do. We feel our cells infused with our personal vitality and charisma radiating into our will and through our physical bodies.

Quick Reference

- Inspires good leadership
- Radiates charisma
- Promotes full participation
- Infuses direction

Red larkspur essence helps us to shift by providing us with greater possibilities. We feel free from the usual limitations of lethargy, apathy, and hesitation. We feel that we are easily able to move beyond our usual default buttons — with great style and flair.

Saguaro

Saguaro

> **Quick Reference**
> - Reveals intentions of traditions
> - Manages feelings of rebellion
> - Embraces wisdom
> - Fosters freedom

Saguaro is tailor-made for feelings of rebellion and isolation. When we want to buck tradition and do things on our own, this essence can help. It does so by showing us how to see beyond our immediate reactions to tradition, helping us to feel the real intention behind a tradition or culture. In other words, it helps us to shift from the confines of our traditions and make peace with our personal pasts. Saguaro has a way of helping us to remember the gifts of our ancestral patterns.

Snapdragon

> **Quick Reference**
> - Softens speech delivery
> - Soothes throat tension
> - Fosters clear communication
> - Helps with TMJ, teeth grinding

Snapdragon essence is used for the snappy and snarky among us. We can't help it! We can't help but spew venom when people ask us stupidly obvious questions or even just ask for directions. We can't help but point out to people the err of their questions or their ways, taking it upon ourselves to set them straight. And some of us believe

Snapdragon

ourselves to be helpful rather than harsh. We might think that we are being clever, but we get mixed reviews about what we say and how we say it. Then we try to hold back the criticism or biting words but end up grinding our teeth, or even getting temporomandibular joint disorder (TMJ), because we have such a powerful need to express ourselves.

Snapdragon softens the delivery of our voices and words. This remedy helps to channel the creative energy of our words and voices into a more positive expression. We then use our words to create rather than criticize. It is also effective for creative blocks and TMJ, since it releases the tension trapped in the throat area. Snapdragon essence clears us to be true to our own voices and satisfies the itch to react with the screeching and scratchy words.

This essence helps us to release all the pent-up energy in the throat chakra. It cleanses and clears the stuck words. It frees us to vividly express ourselves. Snapdragon transmutes tension into active creativity. It helps to relax the tension and the need to express ourselves in such an aggressive manner so that all of the force that holds us back can now propel us into the future. It helps our words have passion, clarity, and creative expression.

Tansy

Tansy

Tansy essence is what I consider to be the "lazy boy" remedy. Sometimes we don't feel like going anywhere or doing anything, and it takes a lot of effort to complete a little task. At times, we feel like we are just getting by, and we don't really care. We feel the world will wait for us. As a result, we feel stuck by the burden of not doing. Then it makes it even harder to get moving because our get-up-and-go got up and left. Worst of all, we can't figure out how that happened. Tansy essence is not so much about the get-up-and-go; it's more about tapping into purpose and filling meaningful goals. It adds a sense of accomplishment along with the pleasure that comes from following through. It moves our energy in a positive direction.

Quick Reference

- Stops procrastination
- Breaks lazy habits
- Promotes follow-through
- Directs focus
- Provides motivation

Sometimes we sit on things that we know we should be doing. This is a form of controlling our environments in order to do things at our own pace and in our own time. Tansy works by stimulating our feelings of strength and purpose. Energy comes from that strength and purpose, from feeling plugged into something larger than ourselves. Tansy essence is often used in manifestation formulas for its ability to get a person started. It does so in a soft and gentle manner so that we feel we are being motivated from within. Tansy essence shifts us back into gear so that we finally feel ready to make some effort and gain some traction. It springs us forward by connecting us with our innate strength and purpose.

Tansy essence addresses those of us who procrastinate, drag our feet, and have no particular investment in any future events or moving forward in any way. We feel stuck or stymied in the feeling of ho-hum boredom. At times, we choose some misguided means of safety in place of a focused sense of security. Tansy essence rallies our forces. It has the ability to make it safe to be ourselves. It helps us to pull our heads out of the self-imposed shell of then into the conscious participation of now.

Whether we want to do a project or not, Tansy helps us to get started. With this essence, we find ourselves getting off our butts without even knowing how we overcame our own resistance. It leapfrogs us over and through those invisible humps and aids us in creating value for our actions. We do things because we want to, not because of some external pressure. We realize how commitment works for us. We no longer feel overwhelmed by what we have to do, because now we want to participate.

Trumpet Vine

Trumpet vine essence is typically used for people who have speech impediments, such as stuttering. It is indicated for those of us who find it difficult to get our words out. We know what we want to say but stumble. Whatever comes out just doesn't sound right. We feel nobody wants to listen to us. People ignore us when we speak, or they talk over us. We can't project, and our words fall flat.

Quick Reference

- Improves self-expression
- Helps articulate thoughts
- Gives verbal confidence
- Helps with speech impediments

Trumpet vine essence gives us command over our voices and helps us use our vocabulary. We feel good expressing ourselves through our words. We allow the color, timbre, and personality to come through. Our voices become imbued with power. Using this essence shows us that our words are our wands: When they are used with clarity and intention, they help us speak our truth and change our realities.

Trumpet Vine

I like my clients to use this essence when they have a presentation to give, as it adds some verve to how they present themselves. With this essence, we feel confidence. We trust our words. We feel them working for us. We know what to say and how to say it, and speaking feels good. We are in direct connection to Source. This essence is great for those of us who are writers and speakers, as it helps us to articulate our thoughts and concepts more clearly. Trumpet vine also helps us to speak up for ourselves. It boosts verbal and emotional confidence by harmonizing our voices as instruments for creativity. Our declarations have value and strength. Our freedom comes from the ability to express ourselves.

Walnut

Walnut essence is known as the change agent. Whenever there is a transition — whether it's a job, relationship, or geographic move — walnut essence will protect and provide us with the necessary energy. This remedy helps us to be true to our paths. It fortifies that first step to greater versions of our lives. It doesn't work so much as a catalyst for change but as a partner for the natural progression of soul growth. Walnut essence is what Dr. Bach called the "spell breaker."

Quick Reference

- Works as a partner in natural progression
- Embraces change
- Breaks through illusions
- Eases major transitions

This essence breaks through the illusions of what we feel compelled to create. Are we fulfilling our dreams or are we fulfilling the expectations of others? Walnut essence helps us by recognizing and acting on our personal truths. It can give voice to our personal revolutions and evolutions. It allows us to choose the change in order to grow in our own ways.

Walnut helps us to break our ties to the familiar when we feel the impulse from our higher selves to change. Experiencing constant bouts of doubt and fear is the very indicator that you are on the right path. Walnut essence breaks the spell of self-doubt. We want to be comfortable in and with our changes. Transition, by definition, is the change or alteration of one state to another. Walnut has grounding and centering abilities. It helps us to follow through with our inner imperatives.

Walnut essence is considered one of the breakthrough essences. It breaks the invisible ties that bind us to our pasts and how we think we should be. It shows us the value of our personal paths and supports the emotional stamina required for tremendous change. This essence helps us to stay true to ourselves. It aids us in accessing our life plans, and it helps us move beyond our comfort zones and listen to our destinies. Sometimes we see a new vision or version for ourselves but we get trapped into staying the same. Walnut essence reminds us that growth and transitions are natural progressions. It helps us break the cycle of the fear of change. We feel the trust coming into our psyches rather than the doubt. We feel the call of our life plans. We feel the magic.

CHAPTER FIVE

Love Karma

Love does make the world go 'round. We live for love and love to live. Look in the mirror and be the love you want to share. Be worthy. Allow the love to flow and radiate in all that you do and all that you are.

Agrimony

> **Quick Reference**
> - Promotes emotional honesty
> - Aids in self-expression
> - Releases stuffed-up feelings

Agrimony essence deals with emotional honesty. It lends us freedom of self-expression and teaches us to be more authentic in all that we do. Much energy and anxiety is released as we learn to trust in who we are and what we feel. People who need agrimony essence will go to great lengths to let everyone know how peaceful, together, and "on top of it" they are while secretly churning and burning on the inside. Real peace comes from emotional honesty and being appropriate within each moment.

Use this essence for that stuffed-up feeling. When we want to keep everything on an even keel and enjoy the party, we sometimes tend to suppress our feelings to keep the harmony. We might make jokes and try to keep everything light, even sometimes at our own expense. We don't go deep, and we tend to suffer from feeling that we cannot truly reveal ourselves. These stuffed-up emotions lead to physical stuffiness; we are in denial of ourselves and our symptoms. This essence is especially effective at the onset of a cold or flu — when we are literally stuffed up — and we are trying to pretend that we are fine. We can try this essence when we feel that we are denying our needs and desires. It helps us free our spirits and face our feelings.

This is also a good essence to use when we are trying too hard to be emotionally perfect. It is for those of us who define ourselves as low maintenance. We seem to have no needs. We are there for everyone else. We minimize or invalidate any issues we might have, and we just don't want to be a bother. Agrimony essence is sometimes regarded as the "pleaser" essence. We don't want to fail anyone, so we live to be the perfect embodiment of what others expect us to be. When our idea of being perfect is keeping it all inside and dealing with our own issues ourselves, and if our fear is that someone will see us as less than able or perfect, then agrimony essence helps us to be perfect by being true to ourselves.

Bleeding Heart

Quick Reference

- Soothes broken hearts
- Eases deep loss
- Cleanses the heart
- Beckons pure love
- Reestablishes sense of self

Bleeding heart essence is perfect for what it is named for: a bleeding heart. This formula is used when we feel as if we are going to die of grief or from some other deep emotional loss. This could be a broken heart, a job loss, a difficult move, or an injury. Bleeding heart essence is also used for that feeling of loss that makes us want to hold on tighter for fear of losing the object of our desires. It helps with possessiveness and wanting security from love and loved

Bleeding Heart

ones. This essence is a beacon for the purity of love. It reminds us that to really love something, we have to be willing to let it go.

We know better and go through the motions of trying to move forward and put things in perspective, but we can't seem to get our bearings on how to move forward. We find ourselves focused on what we no longer have as opposed to all the things that we do have. Bleeding heart essence helps by moving us beyond the loss. This essence is useful for the brokenhearted, especially if we felt more attached and possessive regarding our particular situation than we have ever felt before. This essence cleanses and liberates our heart energy to feel safe once again. It resets our emotional capacity for feeling loved and safe.

Bleeding heart essence is often also used for emotional freedom. It is used to form healthier attachments. Sometimes we become so attached to people or concepts that we can't conceive of our lives without them. Bleeding heart cleanses the heart and restore's the integrity of the soul. This essence helps to reestablish that the sense of self is not dependent on who, what, why, and how we are attached to something or someone. Freedom comes from cleansing our hearts and emotions.

Borage

Borage essence is used for the times we need personal courage. It has heart-cleansing properties and also helps to clear away the effects of emotional residue. Emotional residue stifles growth and limits the ability to move forward. Borage essence has a beautiful way of lifting our energy to levels that will support us. We often feel overburdened by the weight of our disappointment and despair. This essence frees us to be ourselves by freeing our hearts.

Quick Reference

- Reinstalls optimism
- Clears emotional residue
- Frees the heart
- Provides hope
- Lends an enlightened perspective

This essence counterbalances the tendency to get bogged down by the weight of the world. Its clarifying nature adjusts our perceptions and frees our hearts to soar. It shifts the focus from "I don't know how I can!" to "Why can't I?" Borage essence fortifies the courage of the heart, letting us step out of the shadows and into the light.

Borage's specialty is to go inside the energy chamber of the heart

Borage

and clear out all the old imprints and patterns of wants, needs, stresses, and distresses. This is the remedy that will help free our hearts. It is an emotional pattern breaker and has the distinct ability to help us start fresh. Borage essence restores our emotional confidence. It brings back the trust in our sense and our sense of trust. Borage essence lifts the heavy heart and regenerates our natural optimism.

This essence can also be a remedy for providing hope. It lifts the burden of discomfort and discouragement. It is effective as a balm for any heart stings, strings, and throbs. I like this essence because it buoys up our emotions not by eliminating toxic emotions but by supporting us through positive change. It helps us to shine even when we don't feel like shining. It raises us above all our trials and tribulations and gives us the needed elevation to see more clearly. Borage essence reinstalls the optimism of love and is great for new starts and new beginnings. It has the capacity to bring a fresh view and renew our resources. It helps us to perceive things from a new and enlightened perspective.

California Wild Rose

California wild rose essence can help when we have lost the lust for life. This essence not only works for those times when everything seems out of our reach but also when we don't care enough to do anything about it. When there is a disconnect in our lives, we lack vitality, and we lack purpose, California wild rose essence reestablishes the

Quick Reference

- Activates life force
- Restores enthusiasm
- Helps find purpose, meaning
- Stimulates motivation

California Wild Rose

connection with what makes us tick, what gives us purpose and meaning. This remedy helps us to jump into our calling.

California wild rose is considered the enthusiasm essence, the missing link for engaging in life and her bounty. It creates success by reinstalling enthusiasm. It is used when we feel numb and apathetic. When we feel this way, we may find it difficult to muster any emotion at all, and we might even shut down. It is as if we have downshifted our life forces into neutral, as if we are still alive but not going anywhere.

California wild rose stimulates the forces of motivation by igniting the will to really live. It brings passion for caring about who we are and what we want to do. What happens to our motivation when we feel like we just don't care or we don't want to get involved? Everything takes too much effort. We just don't want the hassles. We feel ourselves slinking into a passive lifestyle, and we just don't want the attention. This essence stimulates our interest in life so that we feel the pleasure of being, doing, and serving. It makes us feel more real and more alive.

This bravery-inspiring essence gets us aligned with our will and our ability to move forward with love and passion. Most of us may believe that hate is the opposite of love. However, apathy and resignation are truly in opposition to love and desire. Our very vitality depends on how engaged we are with our lives and the very substance of our beings. This essence also helps us to participate in our friendships. It works by breaking down the isolation and apathy that accompany self-involved loneliness. Through its influence, our friendships and relationships become a source of enthusiasm, and we love how friendship makes us feel!

Cerato

Quick Reference

- Gives courage to take action
- Helps us trust gut instincts
- Fosters inner certainty
- Helps make decisions

Cerato essence is fundamentally an essence for anxiety — the anxiety of acting on what is important to us and of trusting ourselves enough to move forward. This essence is used when we need the courage to take action. There are times when we get all the best advice possible so that we can determine what we need to do, but we still don't make the choice to act, and we don't know why. We end up missing opportunities because we just cannot take the leap. We don't know how to turn our possibilities into realities.

Cerato essence shows us how to pay attention to what works best for us. It balances doubt with decision. This essence helps us to trust our gut instincts and our personal abilities to discern information. We no longer have the need to ask others for advice. Cerato essence has the ability to help us link to the wisdom of the heart. It helps us pay attention to our personal cues.

Cerato essence is also sometimes known as the "fool for love" essence. We will do anything to get a particular person; we thrive on the charge of winning someone's favor. Cerato essence helps with the impulse of being distracted by the waiting game — waiting forever for the right time or

Cerato

Chamomile

right result. When using cerato, we may find that we stop waiting for that person to get a divorce, get a job, or realize his or her potential. Cerato essence shows us how to be ready, willing, and able for love by being true to ourselves.

We all have many key insights and strong intuition about things, but the slightest doubt or hesitation from another can often completely throw off our judgment. Cerato essence reminds us that we count. It reminds us that we exist and that our contributions are of value. Nobody knows what we need as well as we do. This essence helps us become aligned with our true selves, affirming that we are on the right path. We feel that inner knowing of the right choice for us.

Chamomile

Quick Reference

- Instills calm
- Eases emotional tension
- Harmonizes energy
- Safeguards wounds

Chamomile essence is a component in the Broken Heart Remedy (see Special Combinations chapter). It is the flower essence version of an emotional Band-Aid. It helps to cover the wound and safeguard it while healing. Chamomile essence works on the heart and more specifically on the solar plexus to restore personal value. It fortifies the core to be loved just as we are. It brings in the sunshine after the emotional gloom and doom.

Chicory

Chicory essence is indicated when we are demanding love and attention. We all want varying degrees of adoration. This is normal. However, chicory essence is used in those times when we succumb to devices for negative attention because we can't get the positive attention we seek. We just need to be the center of attention.

Quick Reference

- Teaches unconditional love
- Deals with neediness, selfishness
- Eases demand for attention

This essence is also helpful for that "with all that I do for you" feeling. It is the formula for conditional love: Love has conditions and requirements, and if they are not fulfilled, love is withheld or withdrawn. We may find ourselves fussing and demanding time and attention because we don't want to spend time alone. Chicory treats the diva who feels compelled to outdo other people for the most attention. If we don't get the right amount of attention, then we will demand it while kicking and screaming and creating all kinds of theatrics. It's all about us!

Chicory reminds us how to love and to give without expecting anything in return. It shows us that there is a "love tax" to every emotional transaction. It works by transforming that selfish need into love given freely and deeply. It helps to shift our energy from itching to be seen and heard to feeling comfortable as we are. Chicory essence helps by changing the frame of reference. It allows for an acknowledgment of others' needs, feelings, and contributions. There is less of a tendency to go for that negative attention. There is more peace in giving people their own space.

Chicory is often regarded as the anti-neediness essence. This essence has a way of making us more lovable in our own eyes, allowing us to see that we are getting what we need from feeling good about ourselves as opposed to lassoing it from another. Give this essence to your teenager when he or she is off on a tangent about how mean or unfair you are. You can even take it yourself when you are acting like an adolescent.

Evening Primrose

Quick Reference

- Weaves love and value
- Adjusts attitude
- Allows full self-acceptance
- Releases feeling unwanted

Evening primrose essence is great for treating the feeling of being unwanted. This is a deep core issue and influences every relationship. If you have never really gotten a hold on what it feels to be truly wanted and desired, evening primrose essence can help you to do a retroactive correction, reweaving your life with love and value. Evening primrose essence is tailor-made for helping us trust our judgment. It can aid us in getting out of those phases of feeling rejected or having the attitude of "reject them before they can reject me." Evening primrose can act as an attitude adjuster.

Evening Primrose

This essence also helps us find what we are looking for. If we are avoiding commitment and connection because we don't know how to go through with these things, this essence provides a template and ongoing foundation to feel safe enough to trust and bond. It releases the pattern of feeling unwanted and locates the missing core of unconditional love.

Evening primrose has a supportive effect. It can warm the heart to entertain another outlook. It helps us to realize that maybe we don't have to be right; maybe our shifts will create other shifts so that we can shift out of our negative feedback loops. Of course, this remedy is not a substitute for good therapy, but it can change the vibration of expectation.

When using this essence, we no longer attract abandonment and rejection. Evening primrose reminds us that we are here for a reason and allows us to move beyond limiting belief systems. This essence helps us to rebuild our core with self-esteem and acceptance. It re-creates our foundation as wanted souls. Evening primrose essence challenges us to move beyond our fear of abandonment and embrace a new way of being. It breaks the cycle of fear of rejection and abandonment by allowing full self-acceptance.

Fuchsia

Quick Reference

- Releases trapped emotion
- Aligns emotional bodies
- Shows it's safe to feel
- Releases need to mask discomfort

Fuchsia essence helps those of us who repress major parts of ourselves in order to maintain a distinct version of reality. When we feel as if we can't cope, our emotions might get out of control or we might be tempted to completely suppress the emotional parts of our beings, which can cause us to acquire physical symptoms. We need fuchsia when we freak out over the most mundane things because we are perturbed about something else — getting a headache whenever we have to pay the mortgage, for example, or getting a headache or a stomachache as a result of not confronting our true feelings.

Often, we would rather go off on a hysterical crying jag or claim we just can't cope rather than admit we are angry with someone or something. Using fuchsia essence is a key to releasing trapped emotion.

Fuchsia

Teenagers greatly benefit from fuchsia essence because of their propensity for emotional roller coasters.

There is a liberation of our vitality when our true emotional bodies are in alignment. With the help of this essence, we feel all of our feelings easily and freely. Fuchsia essence shows us that it is safe to feel and that it is safe and effective to show people all of who we are. When we learn to cope by being more authentic and direct about our hopes and needs, we find that we no longer need to mask our discomfort. Think about how much energy it takes for us to hide and suppress our emotions. Fuchsia essence shows us how to reveal ourselves so that we can be seen and heard.

Hibiscus

Hibiscus essence is traditionally used to get in touch with personal passion. It touches the natural vitality and life force within us. Hibiscus makes us feel more alive and more in touch with our feelings. It gives authenticity to what our senses tell us. I like to use it for creative projects, as it helps to integrate all aspects of the body, mind, and spirit. I like the way it makes you feel about all things. It is one of the essences that brings us to life.

Quick Reference

- Integrates mind, body, spirit
- Fosters sensuality
- Restores vitality
- Accesses passion
- Provides emotional warmth

Holly

Quick Reference

- Opens the heart
- Restores wholeness
- Clears emotional palate
- Raises vibration
- Invites love

Holly essence is one of the all-purpose heart cleansers, opening the heart and reducing the drama of strong anger. Holly essence takes us out of the blinding, out-of-control anger and allows us to put things into perspective. Holly essence cools the heart so that we can determine the source of our discomfort. It transforms anger into compassion and insight. It soothes and smoothes the feelings of separation, injury, and hate that cause us to alienate ourselves from others.

Holly essence is often regarded as the ultimate essence for unconditional love. This essence is a catalyst for transmutation and for the transformation of love. When we have a feeling of discomfort and we know something is not quite right, we can use this essence to clear the pathway for other essences. It helps to clear the emotional palate and helps us to get real with what is right and with what is important for us. This essence is also used as an antidote for other negative emotions such as hate and jealousy. Holly opens the heart to receive love — not just the romantic or common form of love, but the bigger love that makes us great.

This is one of the signature essences to use when you don't know which one to start with. This essence can instill the feeling of being loved by Spirit. We feel the full measure of what it is like to have a deep, encompassing, unconditional love. Holly essence incites us to be strong enough to be soft and invites us to know what it feels like to truly love. It helps us to get what we need from ourselves. We sometimes make the mistake of imagining that we have to show anger and throw tantrums to get people's attention so that our needs can be met: Our anger is the signal of our discontent. Holly essence shows us that we can be seen and heard and have our existence acknowledged without such measures.

Holly works wonders in helping us gain clarity regarding our emotional states. It can clear and cleanse old emotional patterns that may prevent us from believing in ourselves. Holly helps us to remember that such love is our birthright. It guards against the fear of loving and not being loved. It works well for strong negative emotions such as hate, fear, and jealousy — anything that makes us feel cut off from love. Holly neutralizes strong negative emotions. It acts as a bridge to our higher selves and higher consciousnesses. It raises our vibrations to achieve the higher versions of our selves. With its help, we no longer are motivated by the pain. Instead, we feel our connection or at least the willingness to be open to the new and to be open to receive.

Larch

> **Quick Reference**
> - Counters self-doubt
> - Provides confidence
> - Breaks through insecurity
> - Shifts perspectives
> - Inspires to step up

What gets in the way of feeling that we are deserving? First, it is imperative that we feel that we deserve to have a good life. We deserve love, we deserve success, and we deserve good health: All that is good, we deserve. Larch essence is perfect for those times when we don't feel up to a task, even though we are, in truth, more than capable of it. This essence helps us when we continually question our performance by measuring ourselves against impossible standards. It is a great remedy to use when we are filled with self-doubt and lack confidence, when we censor ourselves because we are afraid of being judged harshly, or when we are afraid of doing the wrong thing. Larch essence gives us the confidence to try again and again. Failure becomes a challenge rather than a hindrance.

Larch breaks through the invisible field of insecurity. It doesn't make us scream our own praises, but it does shift our perspectives so that we can see how much we contribute. We will find that we stop comparing ourselves to the accomplishments of others. Instead of coming up with all the reasons why we can't do something, we'll find that we want to participate. We'll feel perfectly capable of stepping up and doing what's necessary. Larch is sometimes regarded as the "just do it" essence.

This essence inspires us to be all that we can be. It helps us with the realization that mistakes are part of any process for success. It reminds

us that we will succeed in our own time and in our own way. This essence helps when we think we are not good enough, smart enough, thin enough, or talented enough. It is as if we can finally look in the mirror and take account of our talents. We begin to recognize ourselves for what special gifts we have to offer and who we are. We feel a liquid confidence fuel our energy fields. We take ownership of who and what we are. Larch essence reroutes our detour into grounded confidence.

Love-Lies-Bleeding

Love-lies-bleeding is the "wounded healer" essence. Its particular powers are to transmute pain and suffering and to share a deep empathetic experience for such pain and suffering. Knowing what it is like to experience the depths of despair and having come through it, we can develop a completely new understanding of how others can survive it. With love-lies-bleeding, we become authentic in our vulnerability and have much to teach others.

Quick Reference

- Transmutes suffering
- Helps in coping
- Connects through shared experience
- Helps move beyond trauma

Love-lies-bleeding essence is indicated for the extremes of pain and emotion when we are pushed beyond our limits, when we feel that circumstances are beyond anything we can possibly envision, and our pain and distress make no sense. It helps us to cope during those situations we don't understand. This essence helps us find meaning in our experiences. We find peace in shifting awareness from one of personalized drama to the transformation of how these experiences can serve us and others. We feel how our suffering can change and inspire.

This remedy doesn't necessarily relieve our pain, but it may give clues or answers to how it might serve a greater good. Whenever we are pushed beyond our comfort levels and far past our limits, we are taken to places we wouldn't normally go. Part of the journey of this remedy is to transform our personal suffering and connect with others through a shared language of experiences. We are no longer limited by our personal traumas and dramas.

This essence helps us to detach from personal pain and open us up to the greater awareness of how it serves us. This shift in awareness helps us to change everything. We are no longer limited by the constraints of our suffering. Love-lies-bleeding essence allows us to heal others as we heal ourselves. It helps us recognize how we share suffering and how we can move beyond any traumatic experience.

Mariposa Lily

Quick Reference

- Fosters positive mothering
- Heals trauma
- Activates greater good
- Helps work through abuse, abandonment issues

Mariposa lily is commonly known as the "mother issue" formula. Was your mother overbearing, absent, controlling, or indifferent? When we are judging our own mothers and feeling that we never quite got what we needed or when we don't know how to turn off our own tendencies to mother and smother others, mariposa lily helps us to correct whatever imbalances exist. This essence has a very nurturing quality. It helps us to fit in. Mariposa lily has a way of making us feel wanted.

This essence is often used for unconditional and planetary love. It is the remedy used for soul abandonment. We can easily forget how connected we are as we become bombarded with all of the images and feelings of the current disconnect in our culture. Mariposa lily essence reminds us in a loving, gentle way how connected we all are. This essence activates the greater good in us. We feel more alive and connected but don't know why or how. We know we have a deep sense of peace and

reverence. Mariposa lily essence helps us to realign with higher and more connected versions of ourselves.

Mariposa lily can be added to any healing formula to catalyze the forces of love and healing energy. It is great for both new and experienced moms as well as for inner-child work, working through abuse, and the overall healing process. It allows us to feel the love and helps us to share it. All love begins from loving ourselves as God would love us. Mariposa lily is a great heart enhancer, as it opens us up to unconditional love. More importantly, it opens us up so that we can love ourselves.

Nicotiana

Quick Reference

- Identifies smoke screens
- Brings peace to the heart
- Breaks addictive patterns
- Thaws icy hearts
- Restores the sacred

Nicotiana is the flower from the tobacco plant. Traditionally used to stop smoking, it is also used to identify where our smoke screens are. As a heart cleanser, this essence works by thawing out the hardness that may surround the heart. We might have an image to live up to, so we appear as we think we are supposed to be rather than as who we truly are. This may lead to feeling more cut off from our authentic selves. We become disconnected to what makes us real and allow our illusions to run rampant. We get numb. Nicotiana essence restores the sacred. It restores the sense of peace that comes from having a true heart. This remedy helps to ground us in reality.

It brings peace to the heart, and it is an effective pattern breaker for any addictive qualities. It helps by removing the "smoke screen," or the numbness, around the heart. Many of us have hardened our hearts so we can continue to function in the world today. This essence helps to thaw the ice around the heart that numbs our feelings. Nicotiana essence reminds us of our natural reverence for life, allowing our hearts to open and embrace our feelings. We become true to ourselves and, in turn, truer to one another. We clear the smoke and allow our hearts to feel the pristine energy. We attain peace by being of peace.

Pink Yarrow

Pink yarrow is the empathy essence. This essence reminds us that compassion doesn't mean dysfunction. Healing is not served by bleeding into the wound, and cross contamination helps no one. This is the essence we use for the times when we don't know where we begin and others end; all we get is a big infected mess. This essence allows us to have the appropriate boundaries for the right situation. Through compassion, we radiate love and healing; we do not absorb pain and strife. Pink yarrow essence dries up that emotional sponginess and reminds us that love and healing come from a place of strength, not a contribution to limitation.

Quick Reference

- Maintains healthy boundaries
- Gives clarity and discernment
- Strengthens emotional core
- Fosters empathy

This remedy helps by having us look at how we value ourselves: Do we only have value when we give our life forces to another? Do we feel as if we have to fix things so we won't feel the pain of others? Pink yarrow essence helps us contain our emotional forces and utilize them for grounding and wholeness. It is sometimes known as the vacuum cleaner essence. We find that we inhale emotional debris so often that it becomes part of us. Using pink yarrow gives us clarity and discernment, and we no longer feel the need to merge in order to connect. In this way, we realize the value of connecting through our strengths rather than our weaknesses.

Part of the healing process is to empower and illuminate the way, not to fix things for others. We become enough by realizing our inner boundaries and abilities. Pink yarrow strengthens our emotional cores. It helps us to operate from loving compassion and allows us to radiate what is needed to others rather than absorbing their energy in order to repair it. This essence allows us to regain the spiritual strength to impart true love and compassion. Pink yarrow helps us to retain healthy boundaries in relationships. We can care and love, but we don't have to deprive our friends of their growth lessons. It helps us support our friends along their journeys. The friendship then becomes a gauge of deep change.

Scarlet Monkeyflower

Scarlet Monkeyflower

Scarlet monkeyflower essence is used to deal with fear of anger and other deep, dark emotions. We are often more afraid of the meltdown than of the anger. This remedy helps us to be honest regarding our feelings, no matter how extreme we perceive them to be. Scarlet monkeyflower helps to take the lid off repression. We can deal with our anger rather than ignore it.

Quick Reference

- Helps deal with anger
- Takes lid off repression
- Releases pent-up emotions
- Fosters healthy expression
- Keeps us from losing control

Scarlet monkeyflower shows us that anger and intense emotion have their place. We can feel deep emotions without losing control. We can feel anger when we are experiencing some type of affront and understand clearly that it is an ally, alerting us to our real feelings. We learn perspective without suppression.

This is often regarded as a "making nice" essence. It helps us when we don't want anyone to see us mad or upset — when we feel the need to conceal our feelings, creating a pressure-cooker effect. This is the essence that is used for that emotional stuffing that causes us to burst out at inappropriate times. Scarlet monkeyflower helps us to be more honest about our feelings. With its help, we learn how to communicate our deeper instincts appropriately. Scarlet monkeyflower essence helps us to recognize the perfection of expressing all our emotions.

Wild Rose

Quick Reference

- Fights submission
- Restores interest
- Revives hope
- Activates healing

Wild rose essence is for those times when we just can't get the feeling of connecting with life. We can see what we are missing. We can see that zest and life force in others, but we cannot seem to rally up — and more importantly, we don't seem to care to. We just can't quite put our fingers on how we got off course. This essence prevents us from detouring into an emotional never-ever land, one that is never-ever happy, never-ever sad — just nothing. It brings in the love, joy, and zest for life.

After a long illness or prolonged disability, oftentimes we can lose the spark that makes us want to keep going — the one that keeps us wanting to see what is going to happen next. Wild rose essence works by enhancing the will to live. It reconnects us with our life forces. It rallies our spirits and helps us become more fully integrated with our bodies.

Perhaps we no longer feel the desire to change things because we have decided they are either too much trouble or beyond our control. So we live a half life, not even longing for something better. This essence is

Wild Rose

an antidote for apathy, used to fight submission. Wild rose essence lifts stagnation and revives the spirit. By using it, we feel that we count. We look around and begin to participate again. I like to call this essence the Rip Van Winkle formula because it wakes us from a deep stupor. Wild rose essence heals by encouraging us to embrace life again.

Wild rose essence helps us to feel what it is like to be ourselves on our best day. It liberates us from the emotional constraints of the past. Rather than focusing on the failures of what hasn't worked in our relationships and how our past defines our future, we stop the process. We allow a fresh start and we are in full participation. We adopt the concept that if we act as ourselves, then the people we attract will be more authentic. Wild rose essence allows us to be ready and able to love because we are more connected to our own spirits.

CHAPTER SIX

Beauty Full

The more we embrace that small, still voice inside, the more we embrace the power of our uniqueness. The ability to be true to ourselves is the key to personal authenticity. The more we are, the more we change into who we are.

Buttercup

Buttercup essence is used for eliminating that artificial gauge of who we are and how we fit in. What may be right for one person is not the standard for another. Buttercup essence reminds us that we all are on unique paths. It is used for the times when we feel like the odd person out. Buttercup directly addresses the distortion of how we view ourselves, such as feeling that no one could possibly love or desire us because of our big ears, small chests, red hair, or anything that doesn't fit the latest and greatest trend. This remedy helps us to embrace and accept our idiosyncrasies. We free ourselves by finding our imperfect perfections.

Quick Reference

- Addresses distorted self-image
- Fosters self-acceptance
- Transforms inner experience of worth
- Strengthens and supports

Buttercup is the perfect essence to use when we feel like a stranger in a strange land. This essence helps us to stop comparing ourselves to others. It gets us over how we think we are supposed to be. We see our talents with new eyes and have an appreciation for the unique thought processes and contributions that only we can make. It challenges us to view our specialness with care and consideration. This essence helps us to factor in our innate gifts and talents. With its help, we see ourselves with different eyes.

I like to use this essence when clients feel as if they are out of step with society. They are the independents, artists, creatives, intuitives, and technogeeks who feel that they don't quite fit in or others don't quite get them.

When using buttercup, we no longer feel so devalued by how we compare to others; instead, we recognize the gifts we have to offer. We may still be outsiders, but our perception of who and what we are changes. We have more access to our own brilliance and radiate our divine light.

Buttercup is a strengthening and supportive essence. It's one of those special essences from which anyone can benefit. In particular, it will help during those times when we are launching a new project or when we feel we are going out on a limb with personal self-exploration. Buttercup essence helps us to transform our inner experience of worth, allowing the struggles that we have with our freckles, moles, blotchy skin, or ample curves to become a welcome part of who we are. We feel the value as we allow ourselves to be defined by personal rather than public standards. We can look in the mirror and smile at what we see.

Dogwood

Dogwood essence is for the times when we need to exude natural grace. It is used when we feel gangly and awkward and not in our bodies. I like to use it when someone needs grounding and ease with the body. It is used for manifestation as well as beauty, as it allows us to be fully accepting of who we are. The more authentic we are, the more we are able to manifest and be beautiful. It connects us with the flow of our bodies.

Quick Reference

- Eases awkwardness
- Restores grace
- Helps us feel comfortable in our bodies
- Fosters self-acceptance

Dogwood

Madrone

Madrone essence is used for those times we're feeling too big, larger than life. We spend X amount of dollars, time, and tears attempting to exercise this or surgically remove that. This essence is for those times when we become so consumed by what our bodies should look like that we don't honor or take care of them. Instead, we berate them, restrict them, and try to tame them. Ultimately, this cuts us off from thc ability to receive anything.

Quick Reference

- Helps make peace with body
- Counters dieting drama
- Fosters body acceptance
- Connects to physicality
- Encourages self-love

Madrone essence helps us to make peace with our bodies as they are. Fundamentally, this is an abundance formula. It trains us to embrace physicality and health. It teaches us that we all have our own special body types and that they are not to be compared to some false idol of perfection. When we have an aversion to the size and shape of our bodies, we deny our very livelihood. This essence can be helpful for severe and chronic dieting and for the times we feel we are not meeting our goals. All we see is "big" and how we don't match media images.

This essence helps us to feel more connected to our own physicality. It gives us ownership and joins us to the abundant aspects of ourselves, and we soon come to have appreciation for our ample bottoms or goddess-like bellies. We see and feel ourselves with different eyes — as God would see and feel us. Madrone helps us accept ourselves. Unfortunately, we zero in on our imperfections, rarely seeing how all of our parts fit together to be a greater whole. We don't often recognize how a little self-love can go a long way in caring more for ourselves and loving others. Be comfortable in your skin. Love the way you move, love the way you look, and love the way you are.

Manzanita

Manzanita

> **Quick Reference**
> - Fosters body appreciation
> - Reminds us of our perfection
> - Integrates physicality with spirituality
> - Connects body to spirit and nature

Manzanita essence is the body essence. It helps us to have a deeper appreciation of all the aspects of the body. It stops the judgment that holds a magnifying glass over our perceived imperfections. Manzanita essence helps us to embrace ourselves as we are. Maybe we don't like the way our bellies look, or we can't stand our toes. At times, we become distracted and consumed by the limitations of our bodies. Maybe we have a little extra here or there, or maybe we have our curls in all the wrong places, but manzanita essence reminds us of our perfection just as we are.

This essence works with the concept of the body as an object, helping us to see the body either as a function to serve spirit or as an imperfect vehicle to liberate spirit from. Manzanita essence helps integrate physicality into a partnership with our spirituality. In order to fuel heaven, we have to feed the earth. This essence is often used when we are stuck in the physical. It helps us tune into our bodies and have more reverence for their needs and requirements. Rather than focusing on the imperfections, insecurities, or limitations of the physical, we make peace and tune into what the messages from our bodies mean.

When you feel at odds with a particular part of your body, you can take a few drops of manzanita and ask your body, or body part, for a message: "What is the message from my _____? What does my _____ want me to know? How does my _____ want to be treated?" You will be amazed by the answers.

Pink Monkeyflower

Manzanita essence reminds us that our bodies are part of our spiritual paths. On Earth, it is difficult to function in one without the other. Manzanita essence reminds us that the body is part of nature. We can't disconnect just because we don't like some of the parts. Manzanita essence helps us to feel more at home in the body. It shows us how to respect the body as a temple of life and love.

Pink Monkeyflower

Quick Reference

- Fosters emotional honesty
- Eases fears of exposure and rejection
- Gives courage
- Opens the heart

Pink monkeyflower essence is for when we have such guilt or shame that we feel we don't deserve any kind of love: We feel unlovable and unworthy. We feel exposed all the time and want to hide our true selves. Pink monkeyflower helps us to be more emotionally honest. This essence is used for the times when we feel we are not good enough — when we are fearful of connecting and befriending others because we don't want them to see the supposed deep-down darkness within us. People feel shame for many reasons, as if we have to hide integral parts of ourselves. Our shame could be as simple as being embarrassed by the type of shoes we were forced to wear as kids. It could also be as complex as a long-held family secret.

The indication for pink monkeyflower essence is that we feel set apart in a very negative way and hide ourselves in our supposed shame. Using pink monkeyflower helps us feel safe to share who we are without the fear of shame. So many of us feel we have to be a certain way to get emotional support. There is a fear of rejection, a fear of ridicule, a fear of not belonging. Pink monkeyflower works with the fear of exposure. It allows us to finally get the sense that it is okay to be who we are. We don't have to feel as if we have something to hide. It is enough to be ourselves. We can acknowledge our strengths, our weaknesses, and our humanity. We feel strong enough to be vulnerable and share who we really are.

Pink monkeyflower addresses the shyness and loneliness of not being understood. Its gift is to give us the courage to take emotional risks. This remedy helps us to open up, allowing us to become strong enough for softness and vulnerability. It lets the love come in to dissolve the mask of shame. Love rather than fear becomes our new protection. Pink monkeyflower helps us to reach out for what we need from others so we can feel the connection and once again feel part of the whole.

Pretty Face

Pretty face essence is used for the times when we don't like what we see in the mirror. This is the "big thighs, bad hair, whittle the middle" essence. No matter what we do or what we think, we still see that big monster or little twerp reflecting back at us. We see what we don't love, never what we do love.

Quick Reference

- Gives new self-perception
- Shifts focus to inner beauty
- Increases self-worth
- Counters plastic surgery addiction

Pretty face essence helps us bridge the appearance gap. We first start by forming a truce with our appearance. Then we are able to look at ourselves and make the decision that maybe our thighs aren't so Shrek-like. They are strong, sturdy, and capable. They get us to where we need to go. Pretty face essence helps us to see ourselves in different terms. Through its influence, we are no longer so defined by the perceptions of how we don't measure up or so focused on what we can't compare to. It gives us fresh perspective, allowing us to be comfortable with ourselves as unique emanations of light and love.

This essence helps to remind us of how all greatness comes from self-acceptance. Look around at media images. The most profound examples of art defy conventional parameters of beauty. Much of what is perceived as beauty and attractiveness comes from having a lot of confidence and chutzpah. What we feel about ourselves is what others see.

Pretty Face

Quince

Quince is used for the challenge of femininity. It addresses how women want to work but also want to stay home with the kids and how we rectify the split. We may find ourselves being too harsh because we think or believe that is what it takes to be strong and get the job done. Quince allows us to be strong and soft at the same time. We don't have to sacrifice our natural flow to be outdated versions of what is feminine and what is masculine.

Quick Reference

- Combines strength with softness
- Accesses loving nature
- Eases career conflicts
- Fosters emotional receptivity

Quince

Redwood

Redwood essence works by strengthening us from the inside. It helps with all structural imbalances and is sometimes called a "chiropractor" in a bottle. It rallies our personal and physical strength. It fortifies our will. It encourages us to stand up to be bigger and better. Redwood essence helps us remember who we are.

Quick Reference

- Strengthens from within
- Provides structural support
- Fortifies will
- Reminds us who we are

Sunflower

Sunflower essence is often regarded as the master essence for asserting our value. It coaxes us to bloom and to be fully radiant. It encourages us to stand tall and just be. We can take this formula before a job interview or an important meeting. It makes us shine in our own right. We access the power of the Sun by being ourselves. When we are in alignment with our "souler" power, we become a force of nature.

Quick Reference

- Inspires radiance
- Bolsters and softens the ego
- Builds self-confidence
- Equalizes energies
- Fosters authenticity
- Restores hope

This essence can be used for both those who feel they are the greatest beings who ever lived on this Earth as well as those who are so afraid to shine that they consciously fade into the woodwork in order to not draw any attention to themselves. When we find that we are minimizing our accomplishments or dressing down to avoid any attention, we may need a

boost of the magnificent sunflower. This essence inspires us to be radiant and to take up our own space. We allow ourselves to be big, brazen, and make no apologies for who we are. This essence has a knack for both bolstering the ego and softening its overactive qualities. It turns up the radiance as needed and turns the blaring ego into warmth and compassion.

Sunflower essence aligns all the subtle bodies. It strengthens and emboldens the energy field, assisting us in listening to our own voices; in effect, sunflower helps us get in touch with trusting our perceptions, our versions of reality, and our authenticity. The stronger we become, the more we will trust ourselves. It brings out the big and beautiful energy inherent in each of us. With its influence, we find ourselves saying, "I can do that! I can be that! I want that!" We begin to value and appreciate our contributions and become more willing to share the essence of who we are.

We can feel sunflower working on a cellular level as it courses through our energy fields. We feel our cells smile with graciousness and gratitude as they fill with the loving warmth of self-love and appreciation. Sunflower doesn't let us get away with false opinions of ourselves. It is the great energy equalizer, supporting us where and when we need to be supported — and kicking us in the butts when we get lazy or self-obsessed.

Sunflower is an innocent and warm essence. I am reminded of when my daughter was three years old and loving who she was. She spun around the room as only small children do and exclaimed: "I just love myself!" So beat on your chest, spin around the room, look at yourself in the mirror, and give yourself a rousing welcome.

Violet

Violet

Violet essence is for the times when we feel lost in the crowd. We sometimes feel too delicate or vulnerable to share ourselves. At times, we might feel that we become lost or overwhelmed by stronger personalities, and we do not want to expose who we are. We know we have warmth inside and true desires to share, but we feel inhibited because we don't want to feel crushed by others. We still don't get to be ourselves.

Quick Reference

- Addresses loneliness, shyness
- Fosters self-acceptance
- Makes involvement safe

This essence addresses the loneliness of appearing shy and reserved. We may not be that way on the inside, but sometimes we appear that way on the outside. Violet essence helps with feeling delicate and fragile. This essence helps us to not feel so bruised by the actions of others. Its gift is acceptance of who we are, the way we are. This essence also has a way of giving us extra time to shine; we feel our warmth unfold in its own time.

CHAPTER SEVEN

Special Combination Formulas

"The action of these remedies is to raise our vibrations and open our channels for the reception of the spiritual self, to flood our natures with the particular virtue we need, and to wash out from us the fault that is causing harm. They are able, like beautiful music or any glorious uplifting thing that gives us inspiration, to raise our very natures and bring us nearer to our souls and by that very act to bring us peace and relieve our sufferings."

—Edward Bach

Broken Heart Remedy

Loss can make us feel lost. We can lose our sense of self and our sense of belonging. Loss makes us feel our souls wilt as if we don't have enough substance to keep us upright and together. I like to use borage along with chamomile and bleeding heart essences as an all-purpose broken-heart formula. This combination of essences tackles that phantom limb of lost love. It reconnects us to the power and value of our own hearts.

Bleeding heart essence is the first component in the Broken Heart Remedy. It addresses the agonizing cracks in the heart — the angst, the longing, the loss — while chamomile soothes the emotional roller coaster. Bleeding heart essence alleviates the "I have just been hit in the stomach by a train" sensation and the "my heart has just been torn to shreds and is now being split into shards" feelings.

Borage essence is the second ingredient in the Broken Heart Remedy. It is an effective heart cleanser. It restores natural buoyancy to the heart. Borage essence uplifts, frees, and lightens the heavy load of emotion. It provides the motion for emotion, giving it a place to go up. Borage brings back a sense of hope and faith, allowing us to feel connected to Source; we feel faith, hope, and love returning.

Chamomile essence is the final component in the Broken Heart Remedy. It is the flower essence version of an emotional Band-Aid. It helps to cover the wound and safeguard it while healing. Chamomile essence works on the heart and more specifically on the solar plexus to restore personal value. It fortifies the core to be loved just as we are. It brings in the sunshine after the emotional gloom and doom.

Divine Connection Formula

One of my personal formulas is called Divine Connection, and it is formulated to assist in connecting with our higher selves. It gives us access to the personal realms of dream, prayer, and meditation. I like to say that it lifts the veil. When we lift the veil, we can see things much more clearly without the cloudiness of all the small and big things that get in the way. The key ingredients for the Divine Connection Formula are lotus, angelica, and Queen Anne's Lace essences.

Angelica essence is the first ingredient in the Divine Connection Formula. It helps us to connect to our guides and angels. This remedy creates a pathway to love and guidance. Angelica essence shows us that we have a living relationship with divine assistance and intuition. It helps us understand that we need to believe in order to receive.

Lotus essence is the second component of the Divine Connection Formula. It alleviates any imbalances in the crown chakra or the energy center, which allows us to connect with the god or spirit within. Lotus enhances our ability to meditate, pray, and feel associated with the divine. We feel our natural inheritance as children of Spirit.

Queen Anne's Lace essence is the final component in the Divine Connection Formula. It enhances our intuition and our ability to trust what we see. This essence filters and clarifies our forces of insight. It balances our capacity to obtain new forms of awareness. Queens Anne's Lace essence supports and grounds our natural clairvoyance as a tool that we can easily and effectively access.

Divine Connection Formula can aid in remembering dreams. It assists in meditative practices by clearing out the cobwebs and helping to dispense with the mind chatter. Focusing and letting go become effortless. It is designed to help us experience reverence for everyday life. Divine Connection is also useful for studying, as it enhances clarity of thought and increases focus. It works well with any task that we need to put our attention to.

Manifestation Formula

What stops us from getting what we want? Is it lack of focus? Lack of chutzpah? Lack of follow-through or initiative? It's time to manifest more effectively. A great manifestation formula is the combination of madia, blackberry, and sunflower essences.

Blackberry essence is the first ingredient in the Manifestation Formula. It is the "get off your butt and get to it!" essence. Blackberry is for breakthroughs and rapid change. It catalyzes anything we do. It translates energy into form. We all have ideas, desires, dreams, and wishes. Blackberry essence makes them real for us. It removes obstacles of thought and organizes the energy to manifest the will to action. This formula gets us out of the purely mental realm and into the realm of action and execution. I love to work with blackberry, as it has the ability to boost other essences as well, so whether we are working with confidence, focus, enthusiasm, or being more decisive, blackberry adds rocket fuel to what we want.

Madia essence is the second ingredient in the Manifestation Formula. It helps to bring what we want into focus. It is indicated for lack of focus and spacy behavior. Madia essence counteracts that scattered feeling by showing us how to prioritize and perceive in a more focused manner. It helps us to train our minds and focus our attention in order to be more productive. We become more centered, allowing our perceptions to work for us rather than against us. Madia essence helps us to focus the spotlight on what we want and how to get it.

Sunflower essence is the last component of the manifestation formula. It is another confidence-building essence. It makes us beam and radiate. Sunflower essence shows us how to commit to ourselves. It gives a touch of warmth, enthusiasm, and passion, allowing us to feel that sense of infectious radiance in all that we do. We feel the sun radiating through all that we focus our attention on. Sunflower essence also regulates when we are overdoing it with attention grabbing and the ego. It reduces the blaring heat of ego into the warmth of enthusiasm for others and ourselves.

Rescue Remedy

Rescue Remedy — sometimes called the Five-Flower Formula — is the emergency formula that is specifically and mindfully designed for all emergency situations. It is comprised of star of Bethlehem, rockrose, impatiens, cherry plum, and clematis essences. It is commonly known as the stress formula.

Rescue Remedy is the first choice for any disaster. Its combination of ingredients addresses the full gamut of shock and trauma. Rescue Remedy brings us back to center. The body's self-healing mechanisms are activated, and all distortions as a result of the shock and trauma are effectively neutralized. We can think about this as a remedy to reset or reboot our internal and emotional resources.

Cherry plum essence is used for those times when we feel that we are losing control. Losing control can mean everything is so overwhelming that we actually faint. It can also be that we are afraid we might lose control over our senses. Cherry plum is for when we lose the ability to determine how we will act or react and the very idea of not knowing makes us even more fearful. This essence helps in those times we feel out of control, as if we could just run down the street screaming. Cherry plum essence helps us to be in the flow of events. It works by assisting us in releasing the pent-up trauma and drama.

Clematis essence specifically addresses the dissociation or dreamlike quality that a crisis can take on. It helps by making the surreal more real. Clematis essence helps to snap us out of it.

Impatiens essence addresses the feeling of needing to act immediately, as time is of the essence. Impatiens essence primes us to deal with our sense of urgency in a crisis. It slows down the mad scramble of the thought process. It relaxes the internal tension that comes from the urgings of "how, where, and why do I need to react next?" This essence works by dialing down the urgent response and relaxing some of the tension.

Rockrose essence is used for dealing with terror, with the all-consuming fear of panicking in a crisis. It's used for those times when we lose perspective because our reactions are so over-the-top. We feel we won't survive and all of our physical reactions escalate until we almost shut down. Rockrose essence restores our ability to react and respond appropriately. We access what we need in order to muster the courage necessary. This remedy gives us access to our internal guidance.

Star of Bethlehem essence is for the shock part of the Rescue Remedy. Whether you freeze in the face of trauma or flee, star of Bethlehem deals directly with the shock waves of energy and emotion. I have had a

personal experience with the power of Rescue Remedy to nullify the shockwave aspect. I was in a hurry (a normal part of daily life) and had my hands full with my purse and various packages. I placed the packages in the backseat of the car and kicked the car door closed with my foot. Not paying attention at the time, I smashed my fingers in the car door.

I immediately experienced that sensation of knowing something is bad but it hasn't quite registered yet. Then I felt the throbbing start and that sense of feeling out of control. I retrieved the Rescue Remedy from my purse and quickly poured some into my mouth. Within seconds, even in my exaggerated state, I could feel a cooling down of the throbbing. I could feel the shockwave subside, and a clearer presence of mind emerged. I could think again instead of just react. I felt that I was in control of my mind and body rather than reacting to the injury. It was a powerful adjustment in my consciousness. This was a big lesson in how quickly shock can blind us and stop us in our tracks.

The Rescue Remedy combination preserves our energies and channels our reflexes to conserve our ability to respond rather than react. We are everyday heroes — even if we don't feel particularly heroic or fly through the air or lift a burning car off of a baby. The very acts of awareness and compassion drive us to push through what holds us back, overcome our fears, and be of service to others. We all feel fear. We all have experienced emergency situations. We all have had drama and traumas. This time-honored Bach formula excels at neutralizing shock and trauma from events beyond our control. It helps to center us when we are in the midst of drama and chaos. We feel its effects immediately.

Yarrow Environmental Solution

Yarrow Environmental Solution's specific job is to shield us. Imagine that we are surrounded by a halo of light. Each trauma, drama, insult, or irritation robs us of or chips away at that perfect protective light coating. With each incident or insult, we receive a chink in our overall glow and vitality. We are no longer smooth and even, and we might feel off balance and out of sorts. Things that would not normally bother us if we had our halos intact now bother us because we don't have that natural layer of protection. Our protective coating is rusty and ineffective. Yarrow Environmental Solution restores our shine and energy, making us intact. What a concept! This solution is the brilliant combination of yarrow, golden yarrow, pink yarrow, arnica, and echinacea flower essences in a seawater base.

Arnica essence is the first ingredient in Yarrow Environmental Solution. It is for emotional and psychological armoring. We may have braced for an injury or some kind of violation and our bodies still retain and remember the shock. Arnica essence smooths out the hard edges. It brings the flow back to our bodies. We feel more relaxed as opposed to bracing for every effect. Arnica essence augments the healing process by interrupting the continued response to emotional pain. It fills in the long-standing grooves, helping us to start again.

Echinacea essence is the second component of Yarrow Environmental Solution. It restores the trueness to self. This is the essence to use when we are feeling disconnected. This essence works well when there have been long-standing challenges to the sense of self. This essence contacts our core integrity and brings back individuality. It fortifies the core and makes us feel more real, focused, and empowered despite all assaults to the senses.

Golden yarrow essence is the third component in Yarrow Environmental Solution. It is indicated for protecting core creativity. Artistic ability and creative insight can get stymied and stifled by outside influences. This is an excellent remedy for creative blocks due to feeling either performance anxiety or as if we are being scrutinized under a microscope.

Creativity and intuitive skills by their very nature require a refined sensitivity to others and to their environment. When there are too many outside or adverse influences, creativity suffers. Golden yarrow essence protects the intentions and integrity of the artist and the intuitive.

Pink yarrow essence is the fourth ingredient in Yarrow Environmental Solution. It is for the emotional sponge. It's used for those of us who are the shock absorbers for everyone in our lives. It's for those times when we would rather take the emotional hit than see those we love suffer. Pink yarrow helps to make clearer boundaries of what is theirs and what is ours. We may feel emotions and intuitions so deeply that we can't figure out whether an emotion or concern belongs to us.

Pink yarrow essence helps us by being that beacon of light that raises us to a higher vibration. It also helps us to bring others up as opposed to feeling dragged down. It assists us to break through old holding patterns due to the misguided loyalty of having to get down into the trenches with everyone we meet. Pink yarrow essence creates discernment for our emotional investments.

Yarrow essence is the final component of Yarrow Environmental Solution. It creates a shield of light, protecting and harmonizing all the energy bodies. It works by filling in or weaving together the energetic matrix that can get damaged due to emotional, physical, or spiritual demands on the soul. Yarrow rebalances the light and restores the flow necessary for life and health. It protects the integrity of the "you" within.

Yarrow Environmental Solution was originally developed by essence-sensitive practitioners to combat the noxious effects of Chernobyl. It creates a fantastic shield of energy and protection. It literally reweaves the aura, or the etheric body, after trauma or any type of damage. It is good to use for allergy and irritation, as it has a way of calming and correcting from the outside in.

Because it was developed to combat the effects of the Chernobyl incident, it is helpful for any type of radiation and for those who have had exposure to the electrical fields of such things as airplanes, x-ray machines, computer terminals, and big appliances. Yarrow Environmental Solution, also known as Yarrow Special Formula, repairs the auric field. It is a great remedy to use on a daily basis, as it is both protective and restorative. It provides a shield of light energy to counteract noxious energy effects.

"[Essences] cure not by attacking the disease, but by flooding our bodies with the beautiful vibrations of our higher nature, in the presence of which disease melts away as snow in the sunshine."

—Edward Bach

Lights of Consciousness

I love working with flower essences. They have helped me learn a lot about myself. They have given me insight into others. I love how working with them continues to reveal precious layers of personal substance and excavate gifts. The manner in which flower essences inspire is the manner in which a flower blossoms.

First, there is the smallest bud, tightly tucked and wrapped. You can try to pry the petals open or you can cut them lose, but they still won't blossom and bloom. They most likely will dry, wither, and die. Flowers need the combination and nurturing of all the elements. They require the right soil so the seeds can grow, they need nutrients and hydration to be fully nourished, and they need the warmth of the Sun to incubate their energy. Flowers also need the air to breathe and communicate.

The bud begins to open and share its fragrance, color, and gifts. It can't be forced. It has to evolve. Flower essences teach us how to evolve. When we use them, we learn how to utilize our elements. They inspire us to nourish and be nourished. We learn how to be of beauty and how to orient ourselves. We acquire internal integrity and structure. Flower essences teach us how to be.

Note that there is a degree of readiness when working with the essences. They *invite* us. The beauty is that if we are not ready or if we make the wrong selection, there are no bad consequences or ill effects. I've also noticed that they help us to find answers by inspiring us to ask the right questions. Flower essences show us what we need, not what we want. They gently guide us to our highest vibration: When we have fear, using flower essences doesn't abolish it; rather, it instills more courage. When we are depressed and feel the gloom of low light, essences shine the way to more light and more insight. When we just don't care, flower essences can inspire us to care about something.

By working with flower essences, we work with ourselves. We are nature, and the flower is the highest vibration of the plant kingdom. They inspire the part of the brain that needs splendor, imbuing us with the essence of beauty.

From the time of the ancients, we have used flowers as inspired medicine. Our ancestors would collect and drink the dew of sacred plants to honor the spirit within. I had my own peak experience with the nature of the essences when walking my dogs on one early sunny morning. There are tall pine trees in the park near our house. The marine layer had recently lifted, and the sun was shining through the droplets of dew on the pine needles with the tiniest of yellow flowers. The combination of the light and the dew created a diamond-like brilliance. I felt such joy surge. I got it! I understood what the essences are: illuminated lights of consciousness. I was awestruck as I felt the profound majesty of the tree. I softly touched the needles and brushed the dew onto my forehead, feeling the blessing of the pine. Pine essence is used for guilt. I felt washed clean of whatever guilt I was feeling at the time. I felt free.

I want you to feel free. I want you to blossom and bloom. I want you to allow yourself to unfold, letting your fragrance, color, and texture flower. I want you to go into whatever bit of nature is around you: your vegetable garden, the trees in a park, a window box of herbs, or a flower bursting from the sidewalk. Take a look and really see. Open your eyes to the beauty and intelligence. I want you to plant new seeds. I want you to grow and thrive. Grow. Blossom. Bloom. Flower. Flourish.

Blossom,
Mary Ann Altamirano Antenucci

Glossary

A

Agrimony • ***Façade***
Works when you feel you are playing to what is expected of you and you don't want to let anyone see how it affects you. You don't want anyone to see you sweat, and you minimize whatever challenge or pain and suffering you may be experiencing. This essence allows you to be honest with yourself and others.

Angelica • ***Guidance***
Accelerates and amplifies your connection to your guides and angels. It facilitates an active relationship with your guides. It provides an extra layer of protection for transformation and healing.

Angel's Trumpet • ***Transformation***
Useful for any profound change or transition, such as birth, death, war, or natural disasters. It helps when there is a severe shock to your reality. It teaches you the value of surrender in the process of major transitions.

Apple Blossom • ***Core***
Helps you get in touch with your core. It eliminates with love what no longer serves you. It restores confident desire.

Arnica • ***Armor***
The energetic first responder for accidents or trauma. It stops the trauma from becoming trapped in the tissues. It also helps to release long-standing trauma from the body and psyche.

Aspen • ***Sensitivity***
Works great for the heebie-jeebies. You don't know why you are fearful, but you are. It works well when you feel something terrible is going to happen. You are sensitive to a fault and have difficulty distinguishing your fear from someone else's. It provides an extra layer of protection.

B

Baby Blue Eyes • ***Innocence***
Opens your eyes to give and receive love. It connects you to the feeling of safety and protection. It restores faith in the goodness of others. It lends the feeling of paternal support.

Beech • ***Tolerance***
Works for irritability and general nastiness. It is specifically used for blame and harshness. It is also useful for allergies due to its ability to soothe energetic intolerance.

Blackberry • ***Unstuck***
Great essence for manifestation. It helps to get you unstuck, especially when you have a goal in mind and everything seems to get in your way. It motivates you to take action and see beyond the obstacles. It brings "wings" to the work.

Black Cohosh • ***Courage***
Indicated when you are caught in self-destructive cycles or abusive situations. It restores your sense of value and courage. It breaks the spell of seductive illusion.

Black-Eyed Susan • ***Suppression***
Works for emotional amnesia. You may find it better to avoid or ignore traumas of the past. You feel it is better out of site and out of mind. This essence allows you to use your experiences as fuel for insight and healing.

Bleeding Heart • ***Broken Heart***
Powerful essence for taking the edge off heartbreaks. It works for any type of loss and restores the inner equilibrium to the heart chakra. This essence gives you the strength and stamina to be willing to open your heart and feel again.

Borage • ***Optimism***
Uplifts the downtrodden energy of a broken heart. It acts as an all-purpose cleanser to wash away the pain of the past and reset the ability to feel light, loved, and cherished. It adds lightness to a heavy heart.

Buttercup • ***Ugly Duckling***
Works when you feel you have differences that make you feel less than. You don't have the same value for who you are and what you have to offer. This essence helps you shine in your own light and in your own time.

C

Calendula • ***Dialogue***
Helps you access the ability to use your words for growth. It installs the power of the word. It softens communication so that the intention behind the words can be communicated and received. It works well when there is a harshness or argumentative quality to expression. It sweetens and soothes communication when you have "that tone."

California Poppy • ***Inner Development***
Helps you develop your spiritual gifts by balancing and listening to your insights for growth. It works when you are attracted to outside spiritual sources for rapid growth and approval. This essence helps you to find the gold within and to secure a trusting relationship to Spirit.

California Wild Rose • ***Apathy***
Teaches you how to show up for your life and how to care. It's primarily used when the life forces are stifled and there is not enough "charge" on the vitality to contribute in your life. This essence can turn your pilot light of love and participation back on.

Canyon Dudleya • ***Discernment***
Indicated when you are attracted to the psychic, mediumistic, and spiritual world at the expense of the mundane world. It helps you to take care of your worldly business to create a foundation for achieving the higher energetic states. It reminds you to do the necessary work for your spiritual gains.

Cayenne • ***Stagnation***
Used as "rocket fuel" for your goals and desires. It catalyzes whatever issues you are working with. It sparks a fire in your belly to believe and achieve.

Centaury • ***Pushover***
Empowers you to be yourself. It teaches you how to stand up for yourself and mean it. It gives you strength and purpose. It is useful when there is a tendency to give until it hurts and then give some more.

Cerato • ***Trust***
Works when you can't trust your own judgment. You have an inkling as to what is right for you; however, you have to collect all the input of all the people instead of following your intuition. This essence challenges you to access your higher guidance and trust what comes through.

Chamomile • ***Calm***
Brings calm and clarity when the emotions are stormy and tense. This essence works specifically for tension in the stomach and solar plexus. It can also create balance in physical upset over power struggles with others. It reduces pent-up bodily tensions. It greatly benefits children who don't yet have the vocabulary to express emotional turmoil.

Chaparral • ***Purify***
Filters toxic emotions and patterns. Cleanses energy imprints from the auric field. It aids in physical, emotional, and drug detoxification. It is beneficial for distressing dreams and nightmares. This is a dream catcher in liquid form.

Cherry Plum • ***Overload***
Works when there is a disconnect with your higher guidance. It's used for that feeling that you can't hold back any longer for fear you are going to explode. It restores your emotional equilibrium.

Chestnut Bud • ***Learning***
Brings awareness to your life lessons and learning. It helps keep you from repeating the same mistakes over and over. It gives you new perspective on what you know and how to use it.

Chicory • ***Possessive***
Works when there is not enough attention, love, admiration, and so on, to go around, so you jealously intercept any attention not coming your way. This remedy teaches conscious and unconditional dedication for the good of all.

Clematis • ***Daydream***
Works when you don't feel engaged or connected to your present state of reality. Dr. Bach considered this state to be a "polite form of suicide." When the dream is more important than the day, this essence helps you engage in reality and inspires your creative juices in the present.

Columbine • ***Individuality***
Helps you to access your creative forces of true self-expression. It makes it safe to be you.

Corn • ***Grounded***
Helps for feeling disconnected and boxed in by your environment. It finds the connection to nature and spaciousness within.

Cosmos • ***Flustered***
Focuses communication. It works well when you have a great idea and can't get it out fast enough. You know what you want to do and what you want to say, but you end up losing the thread and flubbing through your creative concepts. This essence pulls the threads of thoughts to create an articulate, cohesive, and coherent speech.

Crab Apple • ***Perfection***
Works when feeling unclean and struggling with the concept of perfection. This is the "germ phobia" essence. It is used for detoxification and cleansing of the emotional and physical body.

D

Dandelion • ***Tense***
Indicated for internal tension. It helps those who manage their time by filling it with an abundance of activities to distract from listening and self-reflection. This essence gets you back into the flow of life and releases pent-up tension.

Deer Brush • ***Authenticity***
Helps with authenticity. This essence makes your inner and outer motives congruent. It clears your personal denial about who you truly are.

Dogwood • ***Awkward***
Indicated when you don't feel comfortable in your body. You may be accident-prone or lack awareness of what goes where and feel a physical disconnect as if your body belongs to someone else. This essence helps you to feel more fluid and graceful in your physicality.

E

Echinacea • ***Shattered***
Restores and repairs our sense of self after severe abuse and trauma. This essence helps you to pick up the pieces and become whole again.

Elm • ***Overwhelmed***
Works well when you have run out of steam and resources and believe you have nothing else to give. It revives your faith in yourself.

F

Fairy Lantern • ***Immaturity***
Helps you to retain your wonder and innocence but embrace and thrive in the responsibilities of adulthood. It helps you grow up and grow into a fully integrated adult.

Fawn Lily • ***Involvement***
Releases your inner monk from the monastery. It teaches you to share your spiritual gifts and insights for the cosmic evolution of all.

Filaree • ***Details***
Helps you with maintaining the "big picture." It works well for OCD when you have a tendency to get trapped in all the little details at the expense of the overall plan. It lends an accurate sense of proportion and perspective.

Firewood • ***Resurrection***
Helps you to recover when you have been "burned" in any way. You may have been singed by your circumstances and feel you lack the resources to rebuild. This essence helps you rise from your ashes, resetting and elevating your core vitality.

Fuchsia • ***Psychosomatic***
Disguises true feelings and emotions. It helps you identify your patterns of concealment and passive resistance to change. It works by ferreting out the truth of your feelings.

G

Garlic • ***Fortify***
Works as an emotional, physical, and psychic parasite cleanser. It rebuilds and fortifies your internal structure to protect you from unwanted "hijackers."

Gentian • ***Doubt***
Helps you to believe in yourself, your abilities, your friends, and your higher self. It works to dispel doubt and disappointment in the self. This essence repairs your faith.

Goldenrod • ***Peer Pressure***
Deals with "what will people think?" issues. This essence helps when you are so concerned about fitting into the group that you sacrifice your connection to what is true for you.

Golden Yarrow • ***Impressionable***
Helps to protect the essence of who you are. It is indicated for artists and sensitives who can become swayed by the expectations or impressions of others. It fortifies the core connection to the self and self-expression.

Gorse • ***Hope***
Works when you are feeling lonely and hopeless. It helps you dare to dream and shift your energy to open to new opportunities. It gives you the strength to walk through the door.

H

Heather • ***Self-Absorbed***
Addresses "it's all about me" issues. Helps with incessant talking and self-absorption when you feel there is no room for anyone else.

Hibiscus • ***Sensuality***
Makes it safe to be fully expressed creatively and sexuality. It adds warmth and acceptance to intimate connections. It also helps inspire and integrate positive sexuality.

Holly • ***Unconditional Love***
Indicated for the strong emotions of hate, jealousy, anger, suspicion, and distrust. Holly helps you to feel love rather than judgment and disdain. It aids in healing from the long-term effects of a poisoned heart.

Honeysuckle • ***Longing***
Deals with the "everything was so much better when ______" syndrome. It is indicated for those living in the past at the expense of the present and future.

Hornbeam • ***Vitality***
Great for when you feel like you can't face another week or even another minute of the same routine. It refreshes the senses so you can do what you do with a whole new attitude.

Hound's Tongue • ***Analytical***
Great for when you are seeing everything around you only as a function of what it can do for you and how it can be manipulated. It's used when you are feeling separate from the majesty of nature rather than part of it. It lets you feel your connection to nature rather than the mechanics of how it works.

I

Impatiens • ***Impatience***
Good when you feel there isn't enough time and everyone is obstructing your ability to do what you need to do or when you load yourself up with too many tasks. This essence helps you to pace yourself and feel the flow.

Indian Paintbrush • ***Creativity***
Great essence for full expression. It enhances creativity and connection to your source. It is always a component of any manifestation or creativity formula. It activates and raises your consciousness to think and express outside of the box.

Indian Pink • ***Composure***
Helps you maintain your composure when everything is in chaos. It manages the wear and tear on your energy field.

Iris • ***Inspiration***
Raises your awareness to a higher-vibrational perspective. It shifts your awareness from all the muck and mire that you have collected and holds you back, using it as fertilizer for your greatest and fullest expression. This remedy gets you in touch with your need for beauty. It helps by revitalizing and sustaining the higher senses.

J

Joshua Tree • ***Ancestral patterns***
Breaks the cycle of long-standing patterns of abuse, addiction, and predispositions to illness. It helps you utilize the foundation of your ancestors for growth and awareness. It breaks the spell of abuse and misuse of resources.

L

Lady's Slipper • ***Purpose***
Establishes an ongoing flow between your lower chakras and your crown chakra. It aligns you with your purpose. It helps you to walk your talk. This remedy might be alerting you to a new path when you all of a sudden have sore feet or feel uncomfortable in your shoes.

Larch • ***Self-Doubt***
Helps when everyone around you can see how talented or capable you are but yourself. You are afraid to step into yourself and allow yourself to shine. You interrupt every opportunity to believe in yourself.

Larkspur • ***Leadership***
Promotes positive expression for assuming the mantle of responsibility. It inspires you to be of service and to lead by example. It balances the need to be the "boss" with the desire to lead with positive enthusiasm and radiance.

Lavender • ***Soothe***
Soothes the overwhelmed nervous system. It helps you maintain your sensitivity without becoming depleted. It works especially well when tension is centered in the head and neck.

Lemon • ***Refresh***
Cleanses the mind. It balances the cerebral with the imagination. It refreshes and restores inspired thought. It enhances mental focus and is beneficial for learning disorders.

Lotus • ***Higher Consciousness***
Opens your crown chakra to connect with Spirit. It also balances out amplified spiritual perceptions with a grounded and practical experience of the divine.

Love-Lies-Bleeding • ***Anguish***
Indicated for sheer soul torment, this essence transforms your experience of suffering. It doesn't dull the senses but acts to reinterpret your experience of suffering. It helps you move beyond the deep anguish and connect with others through your shared experience.

Lupine • ***Community***
Works with the concept of true community. It focuses the soul on how to be a meaningful contributor to a larger cause. It helps you to further the needs of the group energy rather than the needs of the individual. It also helps to minimize petty turf wars when working within a group.

M

Madia • ***Focus***
Narrows your field of attention in the same manner a microscope or telescope would enable you to see a better picture. It brings a "vision" to your focus. This essence is another component of any creativity or manifestation formula, which helps you to pinpoint your efforts.

Madrone • ***Body Weight***
Works well when you are at odds with your body or body weight. You may diet, have surgical enhancements, or not feel right about how you see yourself. You also may not feel that you deserve to be nurtured and nourished. This essence allows you to receive soul nutrition.

Mallow • ***Sharing***
Works for being fearful of making the first step or stepping out of your comfort zone. It is for those who really want to participate but their feet freeze to the ground or their words come out all wrong, and they shrink back into themselves. It helps make it safe to share who you are with others.

Manzanita • ***Body Issues***
Useful when there is disgust with the body and its functions. You may feel the need to deprive the body to get closer to Spirit. This illustrates that the body and soul are united, and they both have specific and sacred requirements for growth and empowerment.

Mariposa Lily • ***Mothering***
Teaches you how to get the mothering you need. You may not have the mother you always wanted, and this essence has the capacity to retroactively correct the maternal imbalance. It benefits you by giving you the core mother love you need to restore your core sense of belonging.

Milkweed • ***Dependency***
Works when you have a tendency to go unconscious through eating, drugs, or spiritual practices. It helps you to rally your forces and take a stand. It teaches independence and responsibility.

Mimulus • ***Fear***
Works on known fears. It lends you the courage to face your fears by helping you put one foot in front of the other. It also helps when you hide your fears and suffer in silence. It also works well for sweaty palms or pits.

Morning Glory • ***Hangover***
Helps to keep you bright-eyed and bushy-tailed. It is indicated for toxic hangovers. It fortifies the etheric body to protect from energetic hijackers.

Mountain Pennyroyal • ***Psychic hygiene***
Works as a psychic cleanser. It purges contaminated and unwanted thoughts, strengthens the mental body, and enhances positive mental attitudes.

Mountain Pride • ***Warrior***
Activates positive change. It shows you how to stand up for who you are and what you believe. It is also indicated for manifestation formulas as it catalyzes thought into action. It helps you actually take the steps toward your goals.

Mugwort • ***Dream Life***
Integrates your perception of the dream world with your waking world. It helps you gain insight from your unconscious and directs it in a clear and focused way. It balances your dream life with your waking life.

Mullein • ***Morality***
Enhances your moral compass. It strengthens your sense of purpose. It works well when you have a moral dilemma. It helps you to get right with yourself.

Mustard • ***Gloom***
Excellent for mood swings and melancholy. It balances the internal forces of light and darkness. It brings the sunshine back into the energy field.

N

Nasturtium • ***Intellectual***
Good remedy for students after prolonged study. It helps by integrating the practical and experiential life events with the intellectual experiences. It balances the head and the body.

Nicotiana • ***Smoke Screen***
Great essence for releasing a tobacco habit. It has a more profound application in letting the numbness around your heart thaw. It connects you to the true feelings in your heart.

O

Olive • ***Exhaustion***
Works great for utter exhaustion, whether physical or emotional, when everything is just *too much.* It helps restore your energy levels after a long struggle.

Oregon Grape • ***Paranoia***
Best for when you are expecting the worse from others and feeling judged. It helps you shift your energy to receive positive reinforcement rather than hostility. It helps you feel the goodness of others.

P

Penstemon • ***Persecution***
Indicated when you are feeling sorry for yourself and you have had more than your fair share of challenges and difficulties. It works great to relieve the harshness of your experience and lends great resolve and strength. It injects courage in the face of great obstacles. It benefits and blesses you with perseverance and perspective.

Peppermint • ***Thinking***
Stimulates the sluggish brain. It provides fresh clarity and helps by "waking" your perception. It is often used when there is some type of overload on the entire system. It wakes up the senses and makes everything fresh and new. It also benefits your ability to digest new thoughts, new foods, and new ideas.

Pine • ***Guilt***
Helps when you feel responsible for everything. You take the blame and feel shame if someone or some circumstance around you is not doing as well. You are not able to thrive and step into your full expression due to self-criticism.

Pink Monkeyflower • ***Shame***
Helps when you feel that if anything goes wrong, you will be blamed. You have a fear of being exposed or rejected. You don't feel safe and are fearful of showing or sharing your vulnerabilities. This paves the way for love and acceptance.

Pink Yarrow • ***Sponge***
Works for misguided compassion. You may feel it is your mission to save the world, but you often end up fixing it at the expense of your energy. You don't have adequate boundaries and take on what may not be yours to carry. This essence helps you to be more self-contained and staunches the emotional bleeding.

Poison Oak • ***Boundaries***
Works when you have a wide personal-space boundary and are protective of anyone getting too close. It is also indicated when you don't like to be touched at all. This remedy teaches you how to receive the softer parts of yourself. It helps you be strong enough to be vulnerable.

Pomegranate • ***Feminine Balance***
Used for the challenge of the choices for women. It helps women get in touch with and balance their creative impulses through creating projects, creating life, or a combination of both. This essence brings an awareness of how choices are not mutually exclusive but can be staggered to fit the needs of the many phases of a woman's life.

Pretty Face • ***Beauty***
Beneficial when your concept of beauty is distorted. This remedy helps you access the beauty within rather than what culture or fashion may dictate. It helps when you feel you need to do yet another "nip and tuck" to attain your perfect look.

Q

Quaking Grass • ***Group Consciousness***
Indicated when you need to break away from the herd mentality. You have a desire not to go along with the needs of the group and want to break away, to be independent. It helps you to find your identity within the group and outside of the group.

Queen Anne's Lace • ***Clairvoyance***
Removes emotional and spiritual debris to enhance clarity and perceptions. It helps clear the distortions of unbalanced observations and lends more clarity and accuracy to your personal insights.

Quince • ***Strength***
Works when you sacrifice and distort your perception of femininity in favor of strength and power. This can be the toughness essence when you have to present your authority in a commanding way to be taken seriously. It balances the concepts of authority and empowerment.

R

Rabbitbrush • ***Details***
Helps you by maintaining awareness of the requirements of each detail. It simultaneously aids you in blending the big picture with the little picture without becoming overwhelmed in the process. It makes your mind more flexible to keep up with ever-changing challenges.

Red Clover • ***Mass Hysteria***
Good for when you are feeling influenced by group consciousness and you get caught up in a mob mentality. It helps you to retain individuality and composure in emergency situations.

Red Larkspur • ***Radiant Leadership***
Helps you get in touch with the physical expression of personal charisma. It charges up your natural radiance and channels your natural leadership qualities. It powers up your energy to be a full participant in all of your group activities.

Redwood • ***Vitality***
Helps you take a stand and supports your internal and skeletal structures. This essence lends healing and vitality to any restorative program. This remedy also makes you feel aligned and reinforced through your family lineage. It works by accessing the strength and vitality of the ages.

Rockrose • ***Terror***
Works for panic. It is a component of Bach's Rescue Remedy. It brings calm and perspective to emergencies. This essence works well when you have a tendency to "freeze."

Rock Water • ***Discipline***
Indicated when you feel your path to enlightenment is based on deprivation and strict rituals of food, prayer, or devotion. It helps you evoke the intention of your practice and blossom with the flow of spirit.

S

Sage • ***Wisdom***
Encourages you to embrace all the phases of life. It works especially well in life transitions. It helps you use your expertise as tools for making changes. It gives you the peace and perspective to meet any challenges with grace.

Sagebrush • ***Image***
Used for when you present yourself as someone other than who you are. Who are you pretending to be? This essence helps you use your confidence and creativity to be truly authentic and perfect just as you are.

Saguaro • ***Tradition***
Allows you to embrace the wisdom of the past by integrating the gifts into the present and future. It helps you break free from what no longer serves you either through family traditions or religious expectations. It gives you the freedom and wisdom to choose what is right for you and what life you wish to create.

Scarlet Monkeyflower • ***Repression***
Works when you are afraid of your darker nature. You may not want to address or face the shadow side of your nature. This essence can impart the honesty to embrace what you fear by bringing it into the light.

Scleranthus • ***Indecision***
Helps when you aren't able to choose and follow a direction. It's for feeling lost when there are too many choices and all are equally attractive. It's also for not wanting to commit to one choice for fear of losing out on the others.

Scotch-Broom • ***Apocalypse***
Helps when the dire portrayal of world events has you running for your bomb shelter. Take this essence when you want to break the infection of mass hysteria. Better yet, take this essence when you find yourself preparing for the zombie apocalypse.

Self-Heal • ***Healing***
Stimulates the healing process. It helps the body to remember that it can heal. It restores motivation.

Shasta Daisy • ***Wholeness***
Helps you to embrace all of your information — emotional, intellectual, physical, and spiritual — to gain greater insights and a fuller and broader experience of life. It is the life emulsifier, which blends all of your abilities and procedures together.

Shooting Star • ***Disconnected***
Indicated for feeling like a stranger in a strange land. You don't feel connected and have no idea how you can have a sense of belonging. This essence helps you to make sense of who you are and what your place in the universe is. It helps connect you to life on Earth.

Snapdragon • ***Snappy or Snarky***
Helps to clear the throat chakra from tension and aggressive tendencies. It generates clear and creative communication. It helps you to be heard the way you want to be heard. It is also beneficial for TMJ and teeth grinding. It works well to break the habit of sarcasm.

Star of Bethlehem • ***Shock***
Excellent for any type of shock or trauma. It brings the energy back to the present time for healing. It helps neutralize trauma from the past and resets our natural sense of safety and protection.

Star-Tulip • ***Contact***
Helps you to listen and to receive attunements to the higher energies. It is used when you find that it is difficult to contact your higher self due to harshness and rigid interpretations of Spirit.

St. Johnswort • ***Shield***
Works for overexpansion and not being grounded. It helps shield you from disturbed dreams and astral travelers. It protects the solar plexus from power struggles. It protects your innate sense of power.

Sunflower • ***Radiance***
Supports all issues of self-esteem, whether overly confident or, more frequently, not confident enough. This essence lets you bloom into you. It teaches you to be your radiance and shine in your own right. It also works for father issues by restoring a balanced sense of self.

Sweetpea • ***Home***
Used to connect to your inner sense of "home" and what it means to you. It helps when you have moved or move around a lot and lose your inner sense of sanctuary. It restores the feeling of belonging and connection to your environment.

T

Tansy • ***Procrastination***
Indicated when you know you have a lot to do but don't feel like doing it. You may think about trying to muster up some motivation, but you rarely follow through. This essence makes it your idea to be directed and focused. You no longer wait for the motivation mood to strike.

Tiger Lily • ***Competition***
Great for women who feel the need to prove themselves. It helps balance what are perceived as feminine and masculine tendencies. It works on core empowerment rather than power as the need to control.

Trillium • ***Materialism***
Used when you assess yourself and others based on how much you make and what you own. This remedy integrates the spiritual and the material, creating a new, more positive and purposeful foundation.

Trumpet Vine • ***Articulate***
Works well when there is a lack of confidence in verbal expression. It is used for stuttering, any type of speech impediment, or any lack of ability to be articulate. It creates a beautiful flow for your speech patterns.

V

Vine • ***Tyrant***
Works on the true definition of leadership, which is to serve rather than control.

Violet • ***Shyness***
Indicated when you want to share and you want to feel like part of things, but you don't know how to bridge the gap of awkwardness. You feel lonely because you feel uncomfortable in groups. This essence breaks you out of the shackles of shyness and encourages you to venture forth into new connections with others.

W

Walnut • ***Transitions***
Indicated for any life change. It protects you from the fear of change and helps you benefit from the growth of change. This is a freedom essence, which liberates you from whatever has been holding you back, allowing you to embrace your future. It works well for taking the first step or the next step.

Water Violet • ***Aloof***
Indicated when you are feeling separate or apart from others due to education, stature, social class, or generally feeling different. This essence helps to make you feel more connected to others and their concerns.

White Chestnut • ***Mind Chatter***
Works well when you can't let go of a thought or that song from a commercial that keeps ringing in your head. It is also helpful for how we torture ourselves with "shoulda, coulda, woulda" notions.

Wild Rose • ***Resignation***
Indicated when you don't quite feel like giving up but question whether the effort is worth it. It overcomes the lack of hope and restores vitality to the psyche. It installs the joy to counteract the quiet woe.

Willow • ***Resentment***
Indicated when you feel a gnawing bitterness and an inability to forgive. You feel the need to be right, and you hold on to past infractions. This remedy teaches you how to be open to forgive and release the past.

Y

Yellow Star-Tulip • ***Empathy***
Great remedy for teachers and healers cultivating their need to empathetically connect with their students or clients. It helps by expanding awareness for the needs and requirements of others for further growth and healing. It also works well for burnout and feeling hardened by the demands of others.

Z

Zinnia • ***Play***
Restores your sense of play and humor. It works when you get stuck in a certain perception of how an adult is supposed to behave. It balances the tendency to be somber and serious with the ability to laugh at ourselves and find the joy.

Photo Credits

Apple Blossom
Liz West. Apple Blossoms. 4 May 2006. Wikimedia Commons. Accessed 12 June 2013 from http://commons.wikimedia.org/wiki/File:Appleblossoms.jpg.

Baby Blue Eyes
Jnn. *Nemophila menziesii*. 8 May 2007. Wikimedia Commons. Accessed 12 June 2013 from http://commons.wikimedia.org/wiki/File:Flower-center134343.jpg.

Beech
Krzysztof Ziarnek. *Fagus sylvatica*. 15 May 2009. Wikimedia Commons. Accessed 12 June 2013 from http://commons.wikimedia.org/wiki/File:Fagus_sylvatica_flower_kz1.jpg.

Chaparral
Stan Shebs. *Larrea tridentata*. May 2005. Wikimedia Commons. Accessed 12 June 2013 from https://commons.wikimedia.org/wiki/File:Larrea_tridentata_5.jpg.

Cherry Plum
Martinas Angel. *Flori de corcodus*. 27 April 2011. Wikimedia Commons. Accessed 12 June 2013 from http://commons.wikimedia.org/wiki/File:Flori_de_corcodus.JPG.

Corn
Eric1513. Harvest Corn Field. 29 September 2007. Dreamstime. Accessed 3 December 2011 from http://www.dreamstime.com/royalty-free-stock-photos-harvest-corn-field-image3270328.

Crab Apple
Anne Kitzman. Flowering Crab Apple Tree. Big Stock. Accessed 12 July 2013 from http://www.bigstockphoto.com/image-67563/stock-photo-flowering-crab-apple-tree.

Echinacea
Danielle Tremblay. Echinacea Flowers. Big Stock. Accessed 12 June 2013 from http://www.bigstockphoto.com/image-1958960/stock-photo-echinachea-flowers.

Elm
Elena Elisseeva. Green Spring Leaves. Big Stock. Accessed 12 July 2013 from http://www.bigstockphoto.com/image-7968202/stock-photo-green-spring-leaves.

Filaree
Svdmolen. *Erodium cicutarium*. 29 April 2006. IJmuiden, the Netherlands. Wikimedia Commons. Accessed 12 June 2013 from http://commons.wikimedia.org/wiki/File:Erodium_cicutarium-02_%28xndr%29.jpg.

Fireweed
Delphine Ménard. *Chamerion angustifolium*. July 2001. Québec. Wikimedia Commons. Accessed 12 June 2013 from http://commons.wikimedia.org/wiki/File:Epilobe_feuilles_etroites_02.jpg.

Garlic
Trans961. Ramsons (*Allium Ursinum*). Big Stock. Accessed 12 June 2013 from http://www.bigstockphoto.com/image-26362295/stock-photo-ramsons-%28allium-ursinum%29-%28also-known-as-buckrams%2C-wild-garlic%2C-broad-leaved-garlic%2C-wood-garlic-or-b.

Gentian
Martin Fowler. Spring Gentian. Big Stock. Accessed 12 July 2013 from http://www.bigstockphoto.com/image-18516716/stock-photo-spring-gentian.

Goldenrod
Anthony Valois. *Solidago californica*. November 2006. Santa Monica Mountains National Recreation Area, California. Wikimedia Commons. Accessed 12 June 2013 from http://commons.wikimedia.org/wiki/File:Solidagocalifornica.jpg.

Golden Yarrow
Alberto Salguero. *Achillea filipendulina*. 4 February 2005. Wikimedia Commons. Accessed 12 June 2013 from http://commons.wikimedia.org/wiki/File:Achillea_filipendula_cap%C3%ADtulos.jpg.

Heather
Willow. *Calluna vulgaris*. 10 August 2007. Near Schneverdingen, Lower Saxony, Germany. Wikimedia Commons. Accessed 12 June 2013 from http://commons.wikimedia.org/wiki/File:Calluna_vulgaris_005.jpg.

Honeysuckle
Meneerke bloem. *Lonicera caprifolium*. 19 May 2011. Wikimedia Commons. Accessed 12 June 2013 from http://commons.wikimedia.org/wiki/File:Lonicera_caprifolium002.jpg.

Hound's Tongue
Walter Siegmund. *Cynoglossum grande*. 31 May 2012. Wikimedia Commons. Accessed 12 June 2013 from http://commons.wikimedia.org/wiki/File:Cynoglossum_grande_8048.JPG.

Indian Pink
Gary M. Stolz. Indian Pink Flower. 27 February 2013. Wikimedia Commons. Accessed 12 June 2013 from http://commons.wikimedia.org/wiki/File:Indian_pink_flower.jpg.

Lady's Slipper
Fai Wong. Deep Red Lady Slipper (Orchid). Big Stock. Accessed 9 July 2013 from http://www.bigstockphoto.com/image-1557037/stock-photo-deep-red-lady-slipper-%28orchid%29.

Lavender
Linnea. Lavender Flower. Big Stock. Accessed 9 July 2013 from http://www.bigstockphoto.com/image-1854311/stock-photo-lavender-flower.

Lemon
Lehava Maghar. Lemon Tree Blossoms. March 2013. Wikimedia Commons. Accessed 12 June 2013 from http://commons.wikimedia.org/wiki/File:PikiWiki_Israel_30943_Lemon_Tree_Blossoms.jpg.

Mimulus
Algirdas. *Mimulus guttatus*. 21 June 2006. Wikimedia Commons. Accessed 12 June 2013 from http://commons.wikimedia.org/wiki/File:Mimulus_guttatus_ziedas.jpg.

Morning Glory
Chan Yee Kee. Beautiful Morning Glory. Big Stock. Accessed 9 July 2013 from http://www.bigstockphoto.com/image-13505546/stock-photo-beautiful-morning-glory.

Mountain Pennyroyal
Stan Shebs. *Monardella odoratissima*. August 2005. Wikimedia Commons. Accessed 12 June 2013 from http://commons.wikimedia.org/wiki/File:Monardella_odoratissima_ssp_pallida_2.jpg.

Mustard
TeunSpaans. *Sinapis arvensis*. 4 November 2005. The Hague, The Netherlands. Wikimedia Commons. Accessed 13 June 2013 from http://commons.wikimedia.org/wiki/File:Herik_17-10-2005_13.59.40.JPG.

Olive
H. Zell. *Olea europaea*. 4 April 2010. Chersonisos, Crete, Greece. Wikimedia Commons. Accessed 13 June 2013 from http://commons.wikimedia.org/wiki/File:Olea_europaea_003.JPG.

Pine
Foxypar4. *Pinus sylvestris*. 14 August 2007. Dornoch, Scotland. Wikimedia Commons. Accessed 13 June 2013 from http://commons.wikimedia.org/wiki/File:Pinus_sylvestris_youngcone.jpg.

Red Clover
Kristian Tuhkanen. Red Clover. Big Stock. Accessed 13 June 2013 from http://www.bigstockphoto.com/image-30312614/stock-photo-red-clover.

Rockrose
Tigerente. *Helianthemum nummularium*. 7 August 2004. Austria. Wikimedia Commons. Accessed 13 June 2013 from http://commons.wikimedia.org/wiki/File:Sonnenr%C3%B6schen.jpg.

Sage
Aomorikuma. Common Sage. 5 June 2004. Aomori, Japan. Wikimedia Commons. Accessed 13 June 2013 from http://commons.wikimedia.org/wiki/File:Common_sage20040605.JPG.

Sagebrush
Stan Shebs. *Artemisia tridentata*. September 2005. Spring Mountains, Southern Nevada. Wikimedia Commons. Accessed 13 June 2013 from http://commons.wikimedia.org/wiki/File:Artemisia_tridentata_2.jpg.

Scleranthus
Der Michels. *Scleranthus annuus*. 5 August 2005. Wikimedia Commons. Accessed 13 June 2013 from http://commons.wikimedia.org/wiki/File:Scleranthus_annuus_IP0505052.jpg.

Self-Heal
Bogdan. *Prunella vulgaris*. 24 July 2005. Wikimedia Commons. Accessed 13 June 2013 from http://commons.wikimedia.org/wiki/File:Prunella_vulgaris_02_bgiu.jpg.

Star of Bethlehem
AigarsR. Spring Flower Star of Bethlehem. Big Stock. Accessed 13 June 2013 from http://www.bigstockphoto.com/image-34716227/stock-photo-spring-flower-star-of-bethlehem.

St. Johnswort
H. Zell. *Hypericum perforatum*. 20 June 2010. Wikimedia Commons. Accessed 13 June 2013 from http://commons.wikimedia.org/wiki/File:Hypericum_perforatum_007.JPG.

Tiger Lily
Stan Shebs. *Lilium humboldtii*. July 2006. University of California Botanical Garden. Wikimedia Commons. Accessed 13 June 2013 from http://commons.wikimedia.org/wiki/File:Lilium_humboldtii_1.jpg.

Trillium
Robert Miner. White Trillium. Big Stock. Accessed 13 July 2013 from http://www.bigstockphoto.com/image-18267740/stock-photo-white-trillium.

Vine
Javier Martin. *Vitis vinifera*. 27 May 2008. Wikimedia Commons. Accessed 13 June 2013 from http://commons.wikimedia.org/wiki/File:Vitis_vinifera_sylvestris_Closeup_SierraMadrona.jpg.

White Chestnut
Aleksey Tugolukov. Blossoming Chestnut Trees. Big Stock. Accessed 13 July 2013 from http://www.bigstockphoto.com/image-45629326/stock-photo-blossoming-chestnut-trees.

Wild Oat
Mykola Velychko. Green Oat. 29 September 2007. Dreamstime. Accessed 3 December 2011 from http://www.dreamstime.com/stock-photos-green-oat-image10585353.

Zinnia
Chalermchai Chamnanyon. Zinnia Elegans Flowers. Big Stock. Accessed 13 June 2013 http://www.bigstockphoto.com/image-40592710/stock-photo-zinnia-elegans-flowers.

CHAPTER 2

Arnica
Walter Siegmund. *Arnica mollis*. 3 August 2008. Wikimedia Commons. Accessed 13 June 2013 from http://commons.wikimedia.org/wiki/File:Arnica_mollis_0035.JPG.

Black Cohosh
Thomas G. Barnes. USDA, NRCS. 2013. The Plants Database (http://plants.usda.gov, 11 June 2013). National Plant Data Team, Greensboro, NC 27401-4901 USA./ Barnes, T.G., and S.W. Francis. 2004. *Wildflowers and ferns of Kentucky*. University Press of Kentucky.

Black-Eyed Susan
Chris Hill. Black-Eyed Susan. Big Stock. Accessed 9 July, 2014 from http://www.bigstockphoto.com/image-8422696/stock-photo-black-eyed-susan.

Centaury
Bernd H. *Centaurium erythraea*. June 2004. Wikimedia Commons. Accessed 11 June 2013 from http://commons.wikimedia.org/wiki/File:Centaurium_erythraea_220603.jpg.

Chestnut Bud
Karelj. The Flowers of Chestnut. Spring 2006. Czech Republic. Wikimedia Commons. Accessed 11 June 2013 from https://commons.wikimedia.org/wiki/File:Ka%C5%A1tan_1.jpg.

Dandelion
Benjamin Gimmel. *Taraxacum officinale*. 26 April 2004. Wikimedia Commons. Accessed 13 June 2013 from http://commons.wikimedia.org/wiki/File:Fr%C3%BChling_bl%C3%BChender_L%C3%B6wenzahn.jpg.

Hornbeam
Jakub Gojda. Hornbeam Leaves. Big Stock. Accessed 11 July 2013 from http://www.bigstockphoto.com/image-26634890/stock-photo-hornbeam-leaves.

Oregon Grape
Syp. *Mahonia aquifolium* flowers and leaves. 21 April 2010. Wikimedia Commons. Accessed 13 June 2013 from http://commons.wikimedia.org/wiki/File:Mahonia_aquifolium_flowers_and_leaves.jpg.

Willow
Anna Kalaschnikow. Macro Shot of Blooming Willow Tree. Big Stock. Accessed 11 July 2013 from http://www.bigstockphoto.com/image-41757781/stock-photo-macro-shot-of-blooming-willow-tree-salix-caprea-summertime.

CHAPTER 3

Angelica
Krzysztof Ziarnek. *Angelica archangelica*. June 2005. Wikimedia Commons. Accessed 11 June 2013 from http://commons.wikimedia.org/wiki/File:Angelica_archangelica_litoralis_inf.jpg.

Angel's Trumpet
Barbara Kelley. Angel Trumpeter Trees. Big Stock. Accessed 11 July 2013 from http://www.bigstockphoto.com/image-12951155/stock-photo-angel-trumpeter-trees.

Aspen
Jerzy Opioła. *Populus tremula*. 18 April 2006. Wikimedia Commons. Accessed 13 June 2013 from http://commons.wikimedia.org/wiki/File:Populus_tremula_1.jpg.

California Poppy
Demmel. *Eschscholzia californica*. 27 March 2008. Wikimedia Commons. Accessed 13 June 2013 from http://commons.wikimedia.org/wiki/File:Eschscholzia_Californica_BluetenUndFrucht.JPG.

Canyon Dudleya
James Conn. Canyon Live Forever. Big Stock. Accessed 12 July 2013 from http://www.bigstockphoto.com/image-32861447/stock-photo-canyon-live-forever-dudleya-cymosa-2.

Columbine
Perlphoto. Columbine Flowers. Big Stock. Accessed 11 June 2013 from http://www.bigstockphoto.com/image-40821763/stock-photo-columbine-flowers.

Deer Brush
Brother Alfred Brousseau. Courtesy of St. Mary's College of California. USDA, NRCS. 2013. The Plants Database (http://plants.usda.gov, 11 June 2013). National Plant Data Team, Greensboro, NC 27401-4901 USA.

Fawn Lily
Thomas G. Barnes. Barnes, T.G., and S.W. Francis. 2004. *Wildflowers and ferns of Kentucky*. University Press of Kentucky. USDA, NRCS. 2013. The Plants Database (http://plants.usda.gov, 11 June 2013). National Plant Data Team, Greensboro, NC 27401-4901 USA.

Gorse
Hans B. *Ulex europaeus*. May 2006. Botanische Tuin TU Delft, Delft, The Netherlands. Wikimedia Commons. Accessed 11 June 2013 from http://commons.wikimedia.org/wiki/File:Ulex_europaeus10.jpg.

Lotus
Peripitus. *Nelumbo nucifera*. 3 February 2008. Wikimedia Commons. Accessed 13 June 2013 from http://commons.wikimedia.org/wiki/File:Nelumno_nucifera_open_flower_-_botanic_garden_adelaide2.jpg.

Milkweed
Brother Alfred Brousseau. Courtesy of St. Mary's College of California. USDA, NRCS. 2013. The Plants Database (http://plants.usda.gov, 11 June 2013). National Plant Data Team, Greensboro, NC 27401-4901 USA.

Mugwort
Easchiff. *Artemisia douglasiana*. 23 June 2006. Wikimedia Commons. Accessed 13 June 2013 from http://commons.wikimedia.org/wiki/File:Artemisia_douglasiana_1.jpg.

Mullein
Shana Schuyler. Mullein. Big Stock. Accessed 11 July 2013 from http://www.bigstockphoto.com/image-2544634/stock-photo-mullein.

Nasturtium
Troyka. Flowers of Nasturtium. Big Stock. Accessed 13 June 2013 from http://www.bigstockphoto.com/image-13327325/stock-photo-flowers-of-nasturtium.

Quaking Grass
Javier Martin. *Briza maxima*. 27 April 2006. Pinos de la térmica, Puertollano, Spain. Wikimedia Commons. Accessed 11 June 2013 from http://commons.wikimedia.org/wiki/File:Briza_maxima2p.jpg.

Queen Anne's Lace
Christian Fischer. *Daucus carota*. 12 July 2011. Wikimedia Commons. Accessed 13 June 2013 from http://commons.wikimedia.org/wiki/File:DaucusCarota.jpg.

Rock Water
Deborah Benbrook. Scottish Stream Running over Rocks. Big Stock. Accessed 13 June 2013 from http://www.bigstockphoto.com/image-13257146/stock-photo-scottish-stream-running-over-rocks.

Scotch-Broom
Hugo.arg. *Cytisus scoparius*. 24 May 2008. Wikimedia Commons. Accessed 13 June 2013 from http://commons.wikimedia.org/wiki/File:CytisusScoparius001.JPG.

Shasta Daisy
Jonathan Billinger. Shasta Daisy. 25 July 2009. Wikimedia Commons. Accessed 13 June 2013 from http://commons.wikimedia.org/wiki/File:Shasta_Daisy,_Leucanthemum_x_superbum_-_geograph.org.uk_-_1419764.jpg.

Shooting Star
Ryan Hagerty. *Dodecatheon meadia*. 1 March 2013. Wikimedia Commons. Accessed 13 June 2013 from http://commons.wikimedia.org/wiki/File:Dodecatheon_meadia_shooting_star_flower.jpg.

Star-Tulip
Bill Bouton. *Calochortus tolmiei*. 1 June 2011. Wikimedia Commons. Accessed 13 June 2013 from http://commons.wikimedia.org/wiki/File:Calochortus_tolmiei_-_Flickr_005.jpg.

Sweetpea
Teun Spaans. *Lathyrus latifolius*. 18 July 2007. Wikimedia Commons. Accessed 13 June 2013 from http://commons.wikimedia.org/wiki/File:Lathyrus_latifolius_Brede_lathyrus_DSCF0405.JPG.

Water Violet
Christian Fischer. *Hottonia palustris*. 20 May 2007. Wikimedia Commons. Accessed 11 June 2013 from http://commons.wikimedia.org/wiki/File:HottoniaPalustrisInflorescence.jpg.

Yellow Star-Tulip
Eric in SF. *Calochortus monophyllus*. 26 April 2009. Wikimedia Commons. Accessed 13 June 2013 from http://commons.wikimedia.org/wiki/File:Calochortus_monophyllus.jpg.

CHAPTER 4

Blackberry
Dawn Endico. *Rubus armeniacus*. 30 May 2005. Monte Bello Open Space Preserve. Wikipedia.org. Accessed 11 June 2013 from http://en.wikipedia.org/wiki/File:Himalayan_Blackberry_%26_Spider.jpg.

Calendula
Wildfeuer. *Calendula officinalis*. 22 October 2006. Wikimedia Commons. Accessed 11 June 2013 from http://commons.wikimedia.org/wiki/File:2006-10-22Calendula05-02.jpg.

Cayenne
Shizhao. *Capsicum annuum*. 17 April 2006. Wikimedia Commons. Accessed 11 June 2013 from http://commons.wikimedia.org/wiki/File:Capsicum_annuum_flower.JPG.

Clematis
Michael Gasperl. *Clematis vitalba*. 10 January 2005. Wikimedia Commons. Accessed 11 June 2013 from http://commons.wikimedia.org/wiki/File:Clematis-vitalba-Waldrebe%28Samenstand%29.jpg.

Cosmos
KENPEI. *Cosmos bipinnatus*. 28 October 2006. Wikimedia Commons. Accessed 11 June 2013 from http://commons.wikimedia.org/wiki/File:Cosmos_bipinnatus7.jpg.

Fairy Lantern
Bill Bouton. *Calochortus albus*. 16 November 2006. Wikimedia Commons. Accessed 11 June 2013 from https://commons.wikimedia.org/wiki/File:Calochortus_albus_-_Flickr_005.jpg.

Impatiens
ArtMechanic. *Impatiens glandulifera*. September 2002. Wikimedia Commons. Accessed 11 June 2013 from http://commons.wikimedia.org/wiki/File:Impatiens_Glandulifera.jpg.

Indian Paintbrush
Christian Mayer. Indian Paintbrush. Big Stock. Accessed 11 June 2013 from http://www.bigstockphoto.com/image-21599921/stock-photo-indian-paintbrush.

Iris
Brother Alfred Brousseau. Courtesy of St. Mary's College of California. USDA, NRCS. 2013. The Plants Database (http://plants.usda.gov, 11 June 2013). National Plant Data Team, Greensboro, NC 27401-4901 USA.

Joshua Tree
Robin Keefe. Joshua Tree. Big Stock. Accessed 11 June 2013 from http://www.bigstockphoto.com/image-3972573/stock-photo-joshua-tree.

Larkspur
Walter Siegmund. *Delphinium nuttallianum*. April 2010. Wikimedia Commons. Accessed 11 June 2013 from http://commons.wikimedia.org/wiki/File:Delphinium_nuttallianum_1824f.JPG.

Lupine
Clarence A. Rechenthin. USDA, NRCS. 2013. The Plants Database (http://plants.usda.gov, 11 June 2013). National Plant Data Team, Greensboro, NC 27401-4901 USA.

Madia
Calibas. *Madia elegans*. 4 October 10. Wikimedia Commons. Accessed 11 June 2013 from https://commons.wikimedia.org/wiki/File:Madia_elegans_flower2.jpg.

Mallow
Sari ONeal. Pink Poppy Mallow. Big Stock. Accessed 11 June 2013 from http://www.bigstockphoto.com/image-47642272/stock-photo-pink-poppy-mallow%2C-callirhoe-alcaeoides-flower-blooming-in-summer.

Mountain Pride
Stan Shebs. *Penstemon newberryi*. April 2007. Wikimedia Commons. Accessed 11 June 2013 from http://commons.wikimedia.org/wiki/File:Penstemon_newberryi_2.jpg.

Penstemon
Thomas G. Barnes, University of Kentucky. USDA, NRCS. 2013. The Plants Database (http://plants.usda.gov, 11 June 2013). National Plant Data Team, Greensboro, NC 27401-4901 USA.

Peppermint
Sten Porse. *Mentha piperita*. September 2006. Kambodscha/Cambodia, Serendipity Beach bei Sihanoukville. Wikimedia Commons. Accessed 11 June 2013 from http://commons.wikimedia.org/wiki/File:Mentha-piperita.JPG.

Poison Oak
Jeff Banke. Poison Oak. Big Stock. Accessed 11 June 2013 from http://www.bigstockphoto.com/image-757732/stock-photo-poison-oak-green-phase.

Pomegranate
Alex Postovski. Twig Blossoming Pomegranate. Big Stock. Accessed 12 June 2013 from http://www.bigstockphoto.com/image-45410098/stock-photo-twig-blossoming-pomegranate.

Rabbitbrush
Matt Lavin. *Chrysothamnus.* 21 September 2005. Wikimedia Commons. Accessed 12 June 2013 from http://commons.wikimedia.org/wiki/File:Chrysothamnus_nauseosus_nauseosus_%284004893056%29_%282%29.jpg.

Red Larkspur
Eric in SF. *Delphinium nudicaule.* 11 April 2009. Wikimedia Commons. Accessed 12 June 2013 from http://commons.wikimedia.org/wiki/File:Delphinium_nudicaule_Lake_County.jpg.

Saguaro
Monica Boorboor. Saguaro Cactus Bloom. Big Stock. Accessed 12 June 2013 from http://www.bigstockphoto.com/image-1574228/stock-photo-saguaro-cactus-bloom.

Snapdragon
Hedwig Storch. *Antirrhinum majus.* 20 July 2008. Wikimedia Commons. Accessed 12 June 2013 from http://en.wikipedia.org/wiki/File:L%C3%B6wenmaul_IMG_6052.JPG.

Tansy
Anna Rutkovskaya. Tansy (*Tanacetum Vulgare*). Big Stock. Accessed 12 June 2013 from http://www.bigstockphoto.com/image-6120541/stock-photo-tansy-%28-tanacetum-vulgare-%29.

Trumpet Vine
Wildfeuer. *Campsis tagliabuana.* 16 July 2008. Wikimedia Commons. Accessed 12 June 2013 from http://commons.wikimedia.org/wiki/File:2008-07-16Campsis_01.jpg.

Walnut
Georg Slickers. *Juglans regia.* 26 May 2005. Berlin, Germany. Wikimedia Commons. Accessed 12 June 2013 from http://commons.wikimedia.org/wiki/File:Juglans_flower_female_20050526_064_part.jpg.

CHAPTER 5

Agrimony
Joan Simon. *Agrimonia eupatoria.* 18 July 2007. Barcelona, España. Wikimedia Commons. Accessed 12 June 2013 from http://commons.wikimedia.org/wiki/File:Agrimonia_eupatoria_04.jpg.

Bleeding Heart
Sreedhar Yedlapati. Bleeding Heart Flowers in the Garden. Big Stock. Accessed 12 June 2013 from http://www.bigstockphoto.com/image-44250742/stock-photo-bleeding-heart-flowers-in-the-garden.

Borage
Yummifruitbat. *Borago officinalis.* September 2005. Wikimedia Commons. Accessed 12 June 2013 from http://commons.wikimedia.org/wiki/File:Starflower_1.jpg.

California Wild Rose
Curtis Clark. *Rosa californica.* 4 July 2006. Pomona, CA. Wikimedia Commons. Accessed 12 June 2013 from http://commons.wikimedia.org/wiki/File:Rosa_californica_2004-07-20.jpg.

Cerato
Wouter Hagens. *Ceratostigma willmottianum.* 25 September 2009. Wikimedia Commons. Accessed 12 June 2013 from https://commons.wikimedia.org/wiki/File:Ceratostigma_willmottianum_A.jpg.

Chamomile
Kallerna. *Matricaria recutita.* 2009. Wikimedia Commons. Accessed 12 June 2013 from https://commons.wikimedia.org/wiki/File:Kamomillasaunio_%28Matricaria_recutita%29.JPG.

Chicory
Pudding4brains. *Cichorium intybus.* 2 September 2006. Denmark. Wikimedia Commons. Accessed 12 June 2013 from https://commons.wikimedia.org/wiki/File:Halvemaanzweefvlieg_wit_%28Scaeva_pyrastri%29_04.jpg.

Evening Primrose
Vitali Dyatchenko. Evening Primrose (*Oenothera*). Big Stock. Accessed 12 June 2013 from http://www.bigstockphoto.com/image-8094484/stock-photo-evening-primrose-%28oenothera%29.

Fuchsia
Diane Deschatelets. Fushia. Big Stock. Accessed 12 June 2013 from http://www.bigstockphoto.com/image-4540806/stock-photo-fushia.

Hibiscus
Paitoon Wisia. Pink Hibiscus Flower. Big Stock. Accessed 12 June 2013 from http://www.bigstockphoto.com/image-46957075/stock-photo-pink-hibiscus-flower.

Holly
H. Zell. *Ilex aquifolium.* April 2009. Karlsruhe, Germany. Wikimedia Commons. Accessed 12 June 2013 from http://commons.wikimedia.org/wiki/File:Ilex_aquifolium_003.JPG.

Larch
Ben Rschr. *Larix decidua.* 17 April 2006. Seelow, Germany. Wikimedia Commons. Accessed 12 June 2013 from http://commons.wikimedia.org/wiki/File:LarixDeciduaFemaleFlower2.JPG.

Love-Lies-Bleeding
Didier Biville. *Amarante Queue-de-renard.* 22 September 2006. Wikimedia Commons. Accessed 12 June 2013 from http://commons.wikimedia.org/wiki/File:Image_005_Amarante_Queue_de_renard.jpg.

Mariposa Lily
Bill Bouton. *Calochortus leichtlinii.* 15 July 2007. San Luis Obispo, CA. Wikimedia Commons. Accessed 12 June 2013 from http://commons.wikimedia.org/wiki/File:Calochortus_leichtlinii_-_Flickr_004.jpg.

Nicotiana
Carl E Lewis. *Nicotiana alata.* 21 July 2007. Wikimedia Commons. Accessed 12 June 2013 from http://commons.wikimedia.org/wiki/File:Nicotiana_alata1By_Carl_E_Lewis.jpg.

Pink Yarrow
Kor!An. *Achillea millefolium var. rubra.* 18 July 2009. Kolomenskoye Park, Moscow. Wikimedia Commons. Accessed 12 June 2013 from https://commons.wikimedia.org/wiki/File:Achillea_%28cultivar%29_03.JPG.

Scarlet Monkeyflower
Curtis Clark. *Mimulus cardinalis.* 17 April 2006. Wikimedia Commons. Accessed 12 June 2013 from https://commons.wikimedia.org/wiki/File:Mimulus_cardinalis_flower_2003-03-12.jpg.

Wild Rose
Kurt Stüber. *Rosa canina.* 28 October 2004. Wikimedia Commons. Accessed 12 June 2013 from https://commons.wikimedia.org/wiki/File:Rosa_canina2.jpg.

CHAPTER 6

Buttercup
Igor Ledić. Buttercup Flower. Big Stock. Accessed 12 July 2013 from http://www.bigstockphoto.com/image-44290183/stock-photo-buttercup-flower.

Dogwood
Stan Shebs. *Cornus nuttallii.* April 2007. Regional Parks Botanic Garden, Berkeley, California. Wikimedia Commons. Accessed 12 July 2013 from http://commons.wikimedia.org/wiki/File:Cornus_nuttallii_4.jpg.

Madrone
Stephen Lea. *Arbutus menziesii.* 20 March 2004. Northern California. Wikimedia Commons. Accessed 12 June 2013 from http://commons.wikimedia.org/wiki/File:PacificMadroneBlossom.jpg.

Manzanita
Walter Siegmund. *Arctostaphylos viscida.* 10 November 2006. Snow Creek Trail, Yosemite National Park. Wikimedia Commons. Accessed 12 July 2013 from http://commons.wikimedia.org/wiki/File:Arctostaphylos_viscida_08198.JPG.

Pink Monkeyflower
Walter Siegmund. *Mimulus lewisii.* 14 February 2011. Wikimedia Commons. Accessed 12 July 2013 from http://commons.wikimedia.org/wiki/File:Mimulus_lewisii_8189.JPG.

Pretty Face
Stan Shebs. *Triteleia ixioides.* April 2007. University of California Botanical Garden, Berkeley, California. Wikimedia Commons. Accessed 12 July 2013 from http://commons.wikimedia.org/wiki/File:Triteleia_ixioides_ssp_scabra_3.jpg.

Quince
Shimizusatsuki. *Chaenomeles speciosa.* 20 March 2008. Near Donglin Temple,Jiujiang, Jiangxi, China. Wikimedia Commons. Accessed 12 July 2013 from http://commons.wikimedia.org/wiki/File:Chaenomeles_speciosa_01.JPG.

Redwood
Ueberwald. *Sequoioideae.* October 2009. Botanical Garden Hermannshof at Weinheim. Wikimedia Commons. Accessed 12 July 2013 from http://commons.wikimedia.org/wiki/File:Urweltmammutbaum_Kurztrieb.jpg.

Sunflower
Bruce Fritz. Sunflowers. 15 February 2005. Wikimedia Commons. Accessed 12 July 2013 from http://commons.wikimedia.org/wiki/File:Sunflowers.jpg.

Violet
Vasta. *Viola odorata.* 13 March 2006. Wikimedia Commons. Accessed 12 July 2013 from http://commons.wikimedia.org/wiki/File:Viole.jpg.

CHAPTER 7

Broken Heart Remedy

Bleeding Heart
See chapter 5 credits.

Borage
See chapter 5 credits.

Chamomile
See chapter 5 credits.

Divine Connection Formula

Angelica
See chapter 3 credits.

Lotus
See chapter 3 credits.

Queen Anne's Lace
See chapter 3 credits.

Manifestation Formula

Blackberry
See chapter 4 credits.

Madia
See chapter 4 credits.

Sunflower
See chapter 6 credits.

Rescue Remedy

Cherry Plum
See chapter 1 credits.

Clematis
See chapter 4 credits.

Impatiens
See chapter 4 credits.

Star of Bethlehem
See chapter 1 credits.

Rockrose
See chapter 1 credits.

Yarrow Environmental Solution

Arnica
See chapter 2 credits.

Echinacea
See chapter 1 credits.

Golden Yarrow
See chapter 1 credits.

Pink Yarrow
See chapter 5 credits.

Yarrow
Alfred Teng. Yarrow Plant Flower Head. Big Stock. Accessed 12 June 2013 from http://www.bigstockphoto.com/image-14527103/stock-photo-yarrow-plant-flower-head.

About the Author

Drawing on vast international experiences, Mary Ann Altamirano Antenucci infuses her knowledge of various healing modalities into her work as a certified spiritual counselor, columnist, and hypnotherapist. She began her career in Western medicine as a lab and anesthesia technician, working with the liver transplant team at the University of California, San Francisco. As a keen student of alternative medical systems, Mary Ann went on to study acupuncture in Singapore. Following her studies there, she began practicing acupuncture and teaching meditation in Saudi Arabia.

She has worked as a writer, publishing the "Flowers that Heal" column for *Awakenings* magazine as well as "Essences of Nature" for the *Sedona Journal of Emergence!* She is a practitioner of energy medicine, holds a third-degree black belt in Hawaiian Kenpo Karate, and has developed and produced her own Fifth Element Essences aura sprays composed of flower essences and essential oils. As a certified spiritual counselor through the American Board of Hypnotherapy, Mary Ann specializes in transpersonal hypnotherapy, timeline therapy, allergy relief, and past-life regression. For more information, visit MaryAnnAntenucci.com.

THE ANCIENT SECRET OF THE FLOWER OF LIFE VOLUME 1

Once, all life in the universe knew the Flower of Life as the creation pattern, the geometrical design leading us into and out of physical existence. Then from a very high state of consciousness, we fell into darkness, the secret hidden for thousands of years, encoded in the cells of all life.

Now, we are rising from the darkness, and a new dawn is streaming through the windows of perception. This book is one of those windows. Drunvalo Melchizedek presents in text and graphics the Flower of Life workshop, illuminating the mysteries of how we came to be.

Sacred geometry is the form beneath our being and points to a divine order in our reality. We can follow that order from the invisible atom to the infinite stars, finding ourselves at each step. The information here is one path, but between the lines and drawings lie the feminine gems of intuitive understanding.

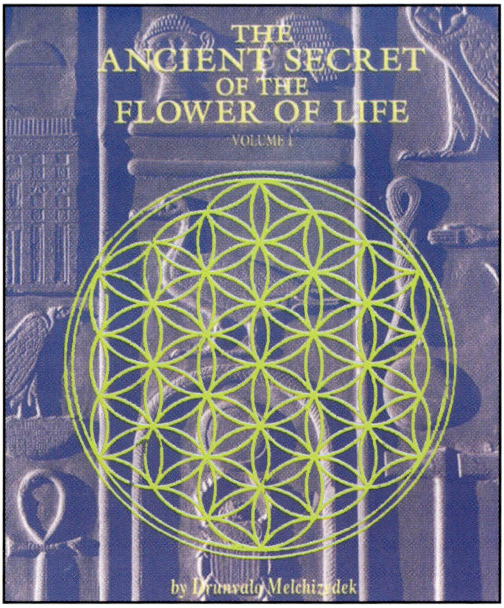

You may see them sparkle around some of these provocative ideas:

- Remembering our ancient past
- The secret of the Flower unfolds
- The darker side of our present/past
- The geometries of the human body
- The significance of shape and structure

$25.00 Softcover, 228 PP.
ISBN 978-1-891824-17-3

Drunvalo Melchizedek's life experience reads like an encyclopedia of breakthroughs in human endeavor. He studied physics and art at the University of California at Berkeley, but he feels that his most important education came after college. In the past twenty-five years, he has studied with over seventy teachers from all belief systems and religious understandings. For some time now, he has been bringing his vision to the world through the Flower of Life program and the Mer-Ka-Ba meditation. This teaching encompasses every area of human understanding, explores the development of humankind from ancient civilizations to the present time, and offers clarity regarding the world's state of consciousness and what is needed for a smooth and easy transition into the twenty-first century.

THE ANCIENT SECRET OF THE FLOWER OF LIFE VOLUME 2

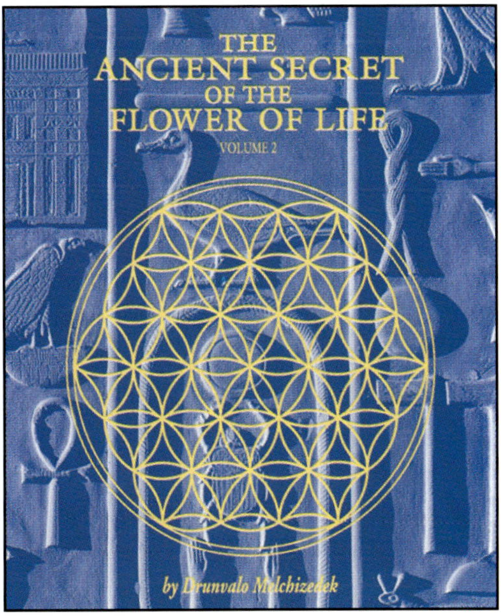

The sacred Flower of Life pattern, the primary geometric generator of all physical form, is explored in even more depth in this volume, the second half of the famed Flower of Life workshop. The proportions of the human body; the nuances of human consciousness; the sizes and distances of the stars, planets, and moons; and even the creations of humankind are all shown to reflect their origins in this beautiful and divine image. Through an intricate and detailed geometrical mapping, Drunvalo Melchizedek shows how the seemingly simple design of the Flower of Life contains the genesis of our entire third-dimensional existence.

From the pyramids and mysteries of Egypt to the new race of Indigo children, Drunvalo presents the sacred geometries of the reality and the subtle energies that shape our world. We are led through a divinely inspired labyrinth of science and stories, logic and coincidence, on a path of remembering where we come from and the wonder and magic of who we are.

Finally, for the first time in print, Drunvalo shares the instructions for the Mer-Ka-Ba meditation, step-by-step techniques for the re-creation of the energy field of the evolved human, which is the key to ascension and the next dimensional world. If done from love, this ancient process of breathing prana opens up for us a world of tantalizing possibility in this dimension, from protective powers to the healing of oneself, of others, and even of the planet.

Chapters Include:

- The Unfolding of the Third Informational System
- Whispers from Our Ancient Heritage
- Unveiling the Mer-Ka-Ba Meditation
- Using Your Mer-Ka-Ba
- Connecting to the Levels of Self
- Two Cosmic Experiments
- What We May Expect in the Forthcoming Dimensional Shift

$25.00 Softcover, 252 PP.
ISBN 978-1-891824-21-0

BY DRUNVALO MELCHIZEDEK

LIVING IN THE HEART

Includes a CD with Heart Meditation

"Long ago we humans used a form of communication and sensing that did not involve the brain in any way; rather, it came from a sacred place within our hearts. What good would it do to find this place again in a world where the greatest religion is science and the logic of the mind? Don't I know this world where emotions and feelings are second-class citizens? Yes, I do. But my teachers have asked me to remind you who you really are. You are more than human being, much more. For within your heart is a place, a sacred place, where the world can literally be remade through conscious cocreation. If you give me permission, I will show you what has been shown to me."

$25.00 Softcover, 120 PP.

ISBN 978-1-891824-43-2

Chapters Include:

- Beginning with the Mind
- Seeing in the Darkness
- Learning from indigenous Tribes
- The Sacred Space of the Heart
- The Unity of Heaven and Earth
- Leaving the Mind and Entering the Heart
- The Sacred Space of the Heart Meditation
- The Mer-Ka-Ba and the Sacred Space of the Heart
- Conscious Cocreation from the Heart Connected to the Mind

Drunvalo Melchizedek's life experience reads like an encyclopedia of breakthroughs in human endeavor. He studied physics and art at the University of California at Berkeley, but he feels that his most important education came after college. In the past twenty-five years, he has studied wizh over seventy teachers from all belief systems and religious understandings. For some time now, he has been bringing his vision to the world through the Flower of Life program and the Mer-Ka-Ba meditation. This teaching encompasses every area of human understanding, explores the development of humankind from ancient civilizations to the present time, and offers clarity regarding the world's state of consciousness and what is needed for a smooth and easy transition into the twenty-first century.

Print books: visit our online bookstore www.LightTechnology.com
eBooks available on Amazon, Apple iTunes, Google Play, and Barnes & Noble

Shifting Frequencies

with CD

Sounds for Vibratory Activation

by Jonathan Goldman

Now, for the first time, Healing Sounds pioneer Jonathan Goldman tells us about shifting frequencies — how to use sound and other modalities to change vibrational patterns for both personal and planetary healing and transformation. Through his consciousness connection to Shamael, Angel of Sound, Jonathan shares his extraordinary scientific and spiritual knowledge and insights, providing information, instructions, and techniques on using sound, light, color, visualization and sacred geometry to experience shifting frequencies. The material in this book is both timely and vital for health and spiritual evolution.

In this book, you will:

- Explore the use of sound in ways you never imagined for healing and transformation.
- Discover harmonics as a key to opening to higher levels of consciousness.
- Learn about the angel chakra and what sounds may be used to activate this new energy center.
- Find out how to transmute imbalanced vibrations using your own sounds.
- Experience the secrets of crystal singing.

$17.95 | **ISBN 978-1-891824-70-8**
Softcover, 147 PP.

Chapters Include:

- Sound Currents: Frequency and Intent
- Vibratory Resonance
- Vocalization, Visualization, and a Tonal Language
- The Harmonics of Sound
- Vocal Harmonics and Listening
- Energy Fields
- Creating Sacred Space
- Compassion through Sound
- Sound, Color, and Light
- Sound and Crystals
- Crystal Singing
- Breath
- The Waveform Experience
- Harmony
- Healing
- The Language of Light

PLANT SOULS SPEAK

A New Way of Interacting with Plants

through Robert Shapiro

"What we intend to speak about — if I may speak in general for all plants — is how you can interact with plants in a more benevolent way for you as the human species. For a long time, you have been clear on medicinal uses of leaves and stems and seeds and flower petals and so on, but you are only getting about one-tenth of the energy available to you that way. It is always better to interact with the plant and its energies in its live form, but you need to know how.

"The intention of this book is to reveal that formula so that you can stop searching, as a human race, for the magical cures to diseases by exhausting the supply of life forms around you when a much simpler process is available. The beings in this book will not just comment on things you know about but show you what you are missing in your interaction with plants."

— Dandelion

$24.95

ISBN 978-1-891824-74-6
Softcover, 520 pp.

Chapters Include:

Cherry Tree	Maple Tree	Palm Tree	Peach Tree
Pine Tree	Redwood	Walnut Tree	Brown Rice
Crabgrass	Oat Grass	Wetland Grass	Angelica
Bamboo	Corn	Daffodil	Dandelion
Hibiscus	Holly	Ivy	Kelp
Marijuana	Orchid	Rose	Sage
Soy Bean	White Rose		

ASTROLOGY

PLANET PERSONALITIES & SIGNS
Speak through Robert Shapiro

12 Planets
12 Signs

PLUS, The Thirteenth Sign and a Planet to Balance Mother Earth

$29.95

ISBN 978-1-891824-81-4
Softcover 674 PP.
6 x 9 Perfect Bound

The Planets and Signs of Astrology speak to us through superchannel Robert Shapiro—sharing not only **LONG-LOST INFORMATION** but also **NEW WAYS OF BEING** for an awakening humanity.

As the Planets and Signs speak through Robert, their personality traits and interests, many of which have been unknown since ancient times, can be clearly heard and felt. In addition, you — humanity — have made such progress that other new energies and traits of the Planets and Signs are expressed through their words. These energies, traits, and characteristics were only potential in earlier times but now are becoming available to you to become aware of and to express within your life on Earth as you awaken to your natural self.

THE HEART OF NUMEROLOGY

by Lynn Buess

Numerology is a symbolic study of rhythms, cycles, and vibrations. In its most esoteric form, numerology simply reflects the tides and cycles of creation as set in motion by the Creator. As it is more commonly practiced, numerology provides a means of understanding cyclical patterns or qualities related specifically to your personal life. By understanding your own particular rhythm, it becomes easier to flow with life. Through the study of numerology, you can become more attuned to your own permanent atom and realign with the dance of the cosmos. With such understanding, you can become the master of fate rather than a victim of destiny's circumstances.

Chapters include:

- The Big Four Primary Numbers
- The Symbolism of Letters
- The Progressed Life Chart
- Name Changes
- The Karmic Lessons of Numbers
- Release Negative Patterns

$25.30 Plus Shipping

ISBN 978-1-891824-97-5
Softcover • 456 PP.
6 x 9 Perfect Bound

Other books by Lynn Buess:

Forever Numerology
ISBN 978-1-891824-65-4
Softcover • 290 PP.
$17.95 plus shipping

Numerology for the New Age
ISBN 978-0-929385-31-0
Softcover • 262 PP.
$11.00 plus shipping

Numerology: Nuances in Relationships
ISBN 978-0-929385-83-7
Softcover • 309 PP.
$13.75 plus shipping

Print books: visit our online bookstore www.LightTechnology.com
eBooks available on Amazon, Apple iTunes, Google Play, and Barnes & Noble

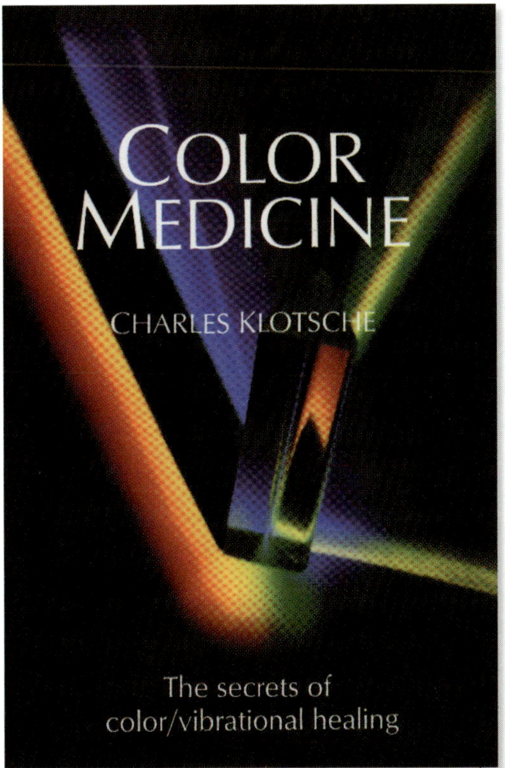

COLOR MEDICINE

The Secrets of Color Vibrational Healing

A new dimension in holistic healing, *Color Medicine* provides a powerful technique for treating specific imbalances and strengthening the immune system. By combining aura-attuned chromatherapy with harmonious sounds, tissue salts, and hydrochromatherapy, the forty-ninth vibrational technique was developed. A breakthrough, yet as old as recorded medicine, it utilizes subtle energy vibrations similar to those found in the visible spectrum. As a textbook and how-to handbook, this book encompasses an encyclopedia of fascinating information, charts, diagrams, and tables, as well as methods of treatment and technical advice. Whether you are a holistic practitioner or merely curious, this book marks a new frontier in the world of alternative healing.

Chapters inculde:

- Does Color Medicine Really Heal?
- Color Physics: The Scientific Explanation of Color Medicine, or Vibrational Therapy
- Color Energetics: How Color Medicine Works with the Subtle Energy Fields of the Body
- Color Harmonics: The Twelve Healing Colors and Their Use
- Color Practice: Materials and Practical Techniques for Applying Color Medicine
- Color Schedule Application: Determining the Appropriate Color(s) for Relieving/Healing the 123 Major Illnesses
- Color Medicine Schedules for 123 Specific Human Disorders
- Quick-Reference Checklist for Color Tonation
- Suggested Readings

$11.95 | ISBN 978-0-929385-27-3
Softcover, 114 PP.

OUT-OF-BODY EXPERIENCES

***by* Gene Schmitz**

WITH CHANNELED EXPLANATIONS AND COMMENTARY THROUGH Robert Shapiro

This book not only tells the full story of Gene's life but it also includes a detailed conversation with an angelic being who speaks through superchannel Robert Shapiro to reveal the meaning behind Gene's out-of-body experiences and his life's purpose. In the process of explaining the twists and turns of Gene's life, this angelic being also unveils some surprising truths about the connection between the body and the soul that apply to all of us.

$14.95
Plus Shipping

ISBN 978-1-891824-95-1
Softcover 144 PP.
6 X 9 Perfect Bound

CHAPTERS INCLUDE:

- Soul Travel Begins
- Soul Travel Continues
- The White Light
- Floating Farther from Home
- My Soul Travels Resume
- Message from Grandpa
- Angels and Animals
- New Traveling Companions
- Soul Crossings

Hearing the Angels Sing:

A True Story of Angelic Assistance

by Peter Sterling

Hearing the Angel's Sing chronicles my extraordinary journeys into the higher dimensions of light where I met the angels who ultimately brought me to the realization that my mission was to be a channel for God's heavenly music. The book includes never-before-shared details of my journey of awakening. From the snowcapped peaks of the Rocky Mountains to the tropical jungles of the Mayan temple lands, to the red rock towers of Sedona, and ultimately to the Incan highlands of Peru, this is a captivating story that will take you on an amazing journey of discovery!

— Peter Sterling

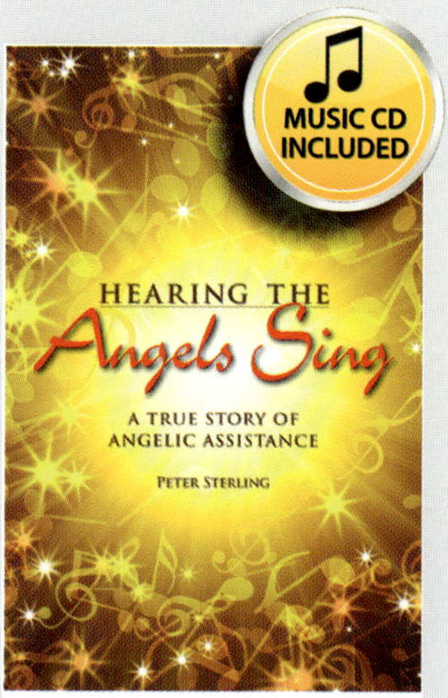

$16.95
Plus Shipping

ISBN 13: 978-1-891824-96-8
Softcover 218 PP.
6 X 9 Perfect Bound

CHAPTERS INCLUDE:

- Descension and Birth
- Down the Rabbit Hole
- Windows to Heaven
- Rocky Mountain High
- Angels and Devils
- Harmonic Converging
- Red Rocks Calling
- To Hear the Angels Sing
- Fires of Purification

DAVID K. MILLER

BIORELATIVITY:
Planetary Healing Technologies

We now accept that human beings are interacting with a living planet, and we understand that this living planet has an energetic relationship to the galaxy. We have also come to understand that the entire biological and energy system of this beautiful planet we live on is totally dependent on how humans treat the planet, the environment, and other life forms on Earth.

Biorelativity describes the ability of human beings to telepathically communicate with the spirit of Earth. The goal of such communication is to influence the outcome of natural Earth events such as storms, volcanoes, and earthquakes. This book is a collection of channeled lectures through Arcturian, Native American, and other mystical guides, transmitted in sessions from 2009 through early 2011, that describe the exercises and thought developments related to biorelativity, the planetary cities of light, and the Arcturian Tree of Life that together form new technology for Earth healing. Through these lessons, you can implement new planetary healing techniques right now, actively participating in exciting changes as Earth and humanity come together in unity and healing.

$16.95

336 pp. Softcover
978-1-891824-98-2

Chapters Include:

- Technologies of Biorelativity
- The Ladder of Ascension over Jerusalem
- Kaballah, Ascension, and the Tree of Life
- Biorelativity and the Immune System
- Cellular and Cosmic Memory
- The Spiritual Technology of Ascension
- Connecting to Your Fifth-Dimensional Self
- Planetary Healing through the Four Bodies
- Istanbul: Sacred Haven of the Eleventh Crystal
- Planetary Spiritual Alchemy
- Aligning with the Arcturian Stargate
- A New Modality of Healing

SEDONA Journal of EMERGENCE!

#1 Channeled Magazine for Spiritual Guidance!

We Offer Answers to Satisfy the Heart and to Inspire Lives!

YOU ARE EXPERIENCING AN UNPRECEDENTED EXPANSION into a new reality and a dimensional shift into a new state of being. This movement from one dimension to another while in a physical body has never been done before. It feels like you are building the rocket you're riding while it is blasting off!

THERE ARE NO ANCIENT BOOKS, NO RULEBOOKS, no manuals or procedures, no record of how to do this thing, because it has never been done before. During previous dimensional shifts, embodied beings would die in the old reality and then be reborn in the new one in new bodies with a different vibrational frequency.

SO LIGHTBEINGS, THROUGH THEIR CHANNELS, EXPLAIN THIS PROCESS and offer guidance and spiritual techniques to help you learn to feel and express love and benevolence — and to encourage you to change your behavior to ensure that Earth remains habitable while you expand into your natural self and awaken to your natural talents and abilities. As this happens, you will allow yourself to flow with all humanity into a more benevolent version of Earth — into another dimensional focus, another of the strata of this existence.

The Sedona Journal of EMERGENCE! is the one monthly magazine readers never throw away.

Get SPECIAL UPDATES of channeled material before it's available on the newsstand with ELECTRONIC SUBSCRIPTIONS!

Print books: visit our online bookstore www.LightTechnology.com
eBooks available on Amazon, Apple iTunes, Google Play, and Barnes & Noble

SEDONA Journal of EMERGENCE!

ORDER ONLINE!
SAVE expensive freight or postage on your *Sedona Journal* subscription

ORDER NOW! TO RECEIVE SPECTACULAR SAVINGS!

We are now making ELECTRONIC SUBSCRIPTIONS

available for the *Sedona Journal of Emergence!*
We have now added content that will not fit into the printed magazine!

- Get the entire journal online by subscription — and get it 2 weeks before it goes on the newsstand!
- Save on expensive freight or postage on your *Sedona Journal* subscription!

Electronic Subscriptions

❒ 1 yr. . . . .$29 ❒ 2 yrs. $55

All Electronic and Combo Subscriptions *MUST* be purchased online at: *www.sedonajournal.com* to obtain username and password

Get the Best of Both Worlds! Special Combo Offers!

USA

Get BOTH Printed AND Electronic Subscription - USA only

1st Class ❒ 1 yr. . . $82 ❒ 2 yrs. . . $159
2nd Class ❒ 1 yr. . . $59 ❒ 2 yrs. . . $109

Canada & Mexico

Get an Airmail Printed Subscription Along with an Electronic Subscription for Only

❒ 1 yr. . . . $95 ❒ 2 yrs. . . . $179

NOTE: The U.S. Postal Service has changed postal rates, eliminating Canadian and global 2nd Class Surface and increasing all airmail rates.

All Countries

Except USA, Canada, & Mexico

Get an Airmail Printed Subscription Along with an Electronic Subscription for Only

❒ 1 yr. . . . $152 ❒ 2 yrs. . . . $285

NOTE: The U.S. Postal Service has changed postal rates, eliminating Canadian and global 2nd Class Surface and increasing all airmail rates.

---

yes! *Send Me:*

USA Printed and Mailed Subcriptions

1st Class	2nd Class
❒ 2 yrs $129	❒ 2 yrs $79
❒ 1 yr $65	❒ 1 yr $43

CANADA & MEXICO

AIR
❒ 2 yrs (24 issues)............ $149
❒ 1 yr (12 issues) $79
U.S. dollars only

NOTE: The U.S. Postal Service has changed postal rates, eliminating Canadian and global 2nd Class Surface and increasing all airmail rates.

ALL COUNTRIES Except USA, Canada & Mexico

AIR
❒ 2 yrs (24 issues)............ $255
❒ 1 yr (12 issues) $136
U.S. dollars only

NOTE: The U.S. Postal Service has changed postal rates, eliminating Canadian and global 2nd Class Surface and increasing all airmail rates.

Name: ____________________

Address: ____________________

City: ____________ State: ______ Zip: ______

Phone: ____________ Email: ____________

Gift Recipient Name: ____________________

Address: ____________________

City: ____________ State: ______ Zip: ______

Personalized Gift Card from: ____________________

METHOD OF PAYMENT:

❒ CHECK ❒ M.O.

❒ VISA ❒ MASTERCARD ❒ DISCOVER ❒ AMEX

CARD NO. ____________________

EXPIRATION DATE ____________________

SIGNATURE ____________________

Phone: 928-526-1345 or 1-800-450-0985 • Fax: 928-714-1132

EASY ORDER 24 HOURS A DAY

1 Order ONLINE!
www.lighttechnology.com
Email:
customersrv@
lighttechnology.net

www.LightTechnology.com
Shopping Cart w/ Secure Transactions
In-Depth Information on Books, Including Excerpts and Contents
Use Our Great Links to Other Sites

2 Order by Mail
Send To:
Light Technology Publishing
PO Box 3540
Flagstaff, AZ 86003

www.SedonaJournal.com
Read Excerpts of Monthly Channeling and Predictions in Advance
Use Our Email Links to Contact Us or Send a Submission
Electronic Subscriptions Available — with or without Print Copies

3 Order by Phone
800-450-0985
928-526-1345

www.BenevolentMagic.com
Learn the techniques of benevolence toward self and benevolence toward others and you will create global peace. Download all the techniques of benevolent magic and living prayer for FREE!

4 Order by Fax
928-714-1132

www.ExplorerRace.com
All of humanity constitutes the Explorer Race, volunteers for a grand and glorious experiment. Discover your purpose, your history, and your future. Download the first chapter of each book for FREE!

Available from your favorite bookstore or:

Light Technology Publishing

MasterCard VISA American Express Discover PayPal

www.ShamanicSecrets.com
What we call shamanism is the natural way of life for beings on other planets. Learn to be aware of your natural self and your natural talents and abilities. Download the first chapter of each book for FREE!

Print books: visit our online bookstore www.LightTechnology.com
eBooks available on Amazon, Apple iTunes, Google Play, and Barnes & Noble